Century 21
SOUTH-WESTERN
Accounting 9E

Multicolumn Journal
Working Papers, Chs. 17–24

Claudia Bienias Gilbertson, CPA
Teaching Professor
North Hennepin Community College
Brooklyn Park, Minnesota

Mark W. Lehman, CPA
Associate Professor
School of Accountancy
Mississippi State University
Starkville, Mississippi

SOUTH-WESTERN
CENGAGE Learning

Australia · Brazil · Canada · Mexico · Singapore · Spain · United Kingdom · United States

SOUTH-WESTERN
CENGAGE Learning

Working Papers, Chs. 17-24, Multicolumn Journal, Century 21 Accounting, 9E

Claudia Bienias Gilbertson, CPA; Mark W. Lehman, CPA

VP/Editorial Director: Jack W. Calhoun

VP/Editor-in-Chief: Karen Schmohe

VP/Director of Marketing: Bill Hendee

Sr. Marketing Manager: Courtney Schulz

Marketing Coordinator: Gretchen Wildauer

Marketing Communications Manager: Terron Sanders

Production Manager: Patricia Matthews Boies

Content Project Manager: Diane Bowdler

Consulting Editor: Bill Lee

Special Consultants: Sara Wilson, Robert E. First

Manufacturing Buyer: Kevin Kluck

Production Service: LEAP Publishing Services, Inc.

Compositor: GGS Book Services

Cover Designer: Nick & Diane Gliebe, Design Matters

Cover Images: Getty Images, Inc.

For product information and technology assistance, contact us at **Cengage Learning Academic Resource Center, 1-800-423-0563**

For permission to use material from this text or product, submit all requests online at **www.cengage.com/permissions** Further permissions questions can be emailed to **permissionrequest@cengage.com**

ISBN-13: 978-0-538-44710-2
ISBN-10: 0-538-44710-9

South-Western Cengage Learning
5191 Natorp Boulevard
Mason, OH 45040
USA

Cengage Learning products are represented in Canada by Nelson Education, Ltd.

For your course and learning solutions, visit **school.cengage.com**

TO THE STUDENT

These *Working Papers* are to be used in the study of Chapter 17–Appendix A of CENTURY 21 ACCOUNTING, 9E. Forms are provided for: (1) Study Guides, (2) Work Together Exercises, (3) On Your Own Exercises, (4) Application Problems, (5) Mastery Problems, (6) Challenge Problems, (7) Source Documents Problems, and (8) Reinforcement Activity 3.

Printed on each page is the number of the problem in the textbook for which the form is to be used. Also shown is a specific instruction number for which the form is to be used.

You may not be required to use every form that is provided. Your teacher will tell you whether to retain or dispose of the unused pages.

The pages are perforated so they may be removed as the work required in each assignment is completed. The pages will be more easily detached if you crease the sheet along the line of perforations and then remove the sheet by pulling sideways rather than upward.

Printed in the United States of America
4 5 6 7 12 11

Name	Perfect Score	Your Score
Analyzing Uncollectible Accts. Expense and Allowance for Uncollectible Accts.	20 Pts.	
Analyzing Uncollectible Accounts Receivable	8 Pts.	
Journalizing Adjustments for Uncollectible Accounts Expense	12 Pts.	
Total	40 Pts.	

Part One—Analyzing Uncollectible Accounts Expense and Allowance for Uncollectible Accounts

Directions: Place a *T* for True or an *F* for False in the Answers column to show whether each of the following statements is true or false.

Answers

1. A business generally sells on account to encourage sales. (p. 514) 1. _____

2. Accounts receivable that cannot be collected are called uncollectible accounts. (p. 514) 2. _____

3. Allowing customers to buy now and pay later is an ineffective method for increasing sales. (p. 515) 3. _____

4. The amount of accounts receivable that is uncollectible is an expense. (p. 515) 4. _____

5. A business usually knows at the end of the fiscal year which customer accounts will become uncollectible. (p. 515) 5. _____

6. Allowance for Uncollectible Accounts is a contra account to its related asset account, Accounts Receivable. (p. 515) 6. _____

7. Recording an estimate of uncollectible accounts to the contra asset account and the expense account is an application of the Matching Expenses with Revenue accounting concept. (p. 515) 7. _____

8. The percentage of total sales on account method of estimating uncollectible accounts expense assumes that a portion of every sales dollar will become uncollectible. (p. 516) 8. _____

9. The adjusting entry for Uncollectible Accounts Expense is recorded at the beginning of every accounting period. (p. 516) 9. _____

10. The adjustment for uncollectible accounts is planned on the work sheet and then recorded in the general journal. (p. 517) 10. _____

11. The adjusting entry for uncollectible accounts does not affect the balance of the accounts receivable account. (p. 517) 11. _____

12. When an adjusting entry for uncollectible accounts expense is recorded, Allowance for Uncollectible Accounts is credited. (p. 517) 12. _____

13. The debit balance of the Uncollectible Accounts Expense account is the estimated uncollectible accounts from sales on account during the next fiscal year. (p. 517) 13. _____

14. When an account is determined to be uncollectible, a journal entry is made to cancel the uncollectible account. (p. 519) 14. _____

15. Canceling the balance of a customer account because the customer does not pay is called writing off an account. (p. 519) 15. _____

16. Allowance for Uncollectible Accounts is debited to write off a customer account. (p. 519) 16. _____

17. Accounts Receivable is debited to write off a customer account. (p. 519) 17. _____

18. When a customer account is written off under the allowance method, book value of accounts receivable decreases. (p. 519) 18. _____

19. Two journal entries are recorded for the collection of a written-off accounts receivable. (p. 521) 19. _____

20. When a previously written-off account is collected, Accounts Receivable is both debited and credited for the amount collected. (p. 523) 20. _____

Part Two—Analyzing Uncollectible Accounts Receivable

Directions: For each of the following items, select the choice that best completes the statement. Print the letter identifying your choice in the Answers column.

1. The loss from an uncollectible account is (A) a liability (B) an expense (C) an asset (D) a reduction in revenue (p. 515)

    1. _____

2. When the percentage of total sales on account method is used, the estimated uncollectible accounts expense is calculated by (A) multiplying total sales on account times the percentage (B) dividing total sales on account by the percentage (C) multiplying total sales times the percentage (D) dividing total sales by the percentage (p. 515)

    2. _____

3. An Allowance for Uncollectible Accounts balance in the Trial Balance Credit column of a work sheet means (A) there are no uncollectible accounts (B) the estimate has not yet been recorded (C) previous fiscal period estimates have not yet been identified as uncollectible (D) equity has been maintained (p. 516)

    3. _____

4. At the end of a fiscal period, the account debited to show the estimated amount of uncollectible accounts is (A) Accounts Receivable (B) Cash (C) Uncollectible Accounts Expense (D) Allowance for Uncollectible Accounts (p. 516)

    4. _____

5. At the end of a fiscal period, the account credited to show the estimated amount of uncollectible accounts is (A) Cash (B) Uncollectible Accounts Expense (C) Accounts Receivable (D) Allowance for Uncollectible Accounts (p. 516)

    5. _____

6. When the allowance account in the Trial Balance column of a work sheet has a credit balance, the amount of the adjustment is (A) deducted from the trial balance amount (B) not recorded (C) estimated (D) added to the Trial Balance amount (p. 516)

    6. _____

7. When the account Allowance for Uncollectible Accounts is used, a customer past-due account is written off as uncollectible by (A) debiting Uncollectible Accounts Expense and crediting Accounts Receivable and the customer account (B) debiting Allowance for Uncollectible Accounts and crediting Accounts Receivable and the customer account (C) debiting Accounts Receivable and the customer account and crediting Allowance for Uncollectible Accounts (D) none of these (pp. 519, 520)

    7. _____

8. To reopen an account previously written off, (A) one general journal entry is recorded (B) two general journal entries are recorded (C) no journal entries are recorded (D) one general journal entry and one cash receipts journal entry are recorded (p. 521)

    8. _____

Part Three—Journalizing Adjustments for Uncollectible Accounts Expense

Directions: In Answers Column l, print the abbreviation for the journal in which each transaction is to be recorded. In Answers Columns 2 and 3, print the letters identifying the accounts to be debited and credited for each transaction.

G—General journal   CR—Cash receipts journal

Account Titles	Transactions	Answers		
		Journal	Debit	Credit
A. Accounts Receivable	1–2–3. Recorded adjusting entry for uncollectible accounts expense. (p. 517)	1. _____	2. _____	3. _____
B. Allowance for Uncollectible Accounts	4–5–6. Wrote off Annie's Place past-due account as uncollectible. (pp. 519–520)	4. _____	5. _____	6. _____
C. Cash	Received cash in full payment of Annie's Place account, previously written off as uncollectible.			
D. Annie's Place	7–8–9. First entry. (p. 521)	7. _____	8. _____	9. _____
E. Uncollectible Accounts Expense	10–11–12. Second entry. (pp. 522, 523)	10. _____	11. _____	12. _____

Study Skills

Participating in Class Discussions

Have you ever been in a class in which one student monopolized the entire class period? Have you ever been in a class in which one student never said a word? Most of us have. Neither the student who speaks too much nor the student who speaks too little is participating in classroom discussion correctly.

No Time for Shallow Opinions

Some students believe that a class discussion is just a time to express personal opinions. However, class discussions should not be occasions where you speak without thinking. No one is interested in hearing a shallow comment or a long discourse that has not been planned.

Prepare Properly

If you know that a discussion will be held during a certain class period, do everything possible to prepare yourself properly. Read the text assignment thoroughly first. Then read any related material that you can find, particularly items in current newspapers and magazines.

Organize your thoughts so that you will be able to express your ideas in a logical manner. When you have thought through the topic thoroughly, you should practice what you will say a time or two. You should then be able to make a convincing argument during the discussion.

Waiting to Speak

In a class discussion, you should spend a great deal more time listening than speaking. If there are 20 students participating in a large discussion group, you probably should speak a total of no more than one or two minutes. If there are only a few students in the group, you may speak a total of five or six minutes.

As you wait your turn to speak, listen carefully to the opinions of others. Many students do not really pay attention to the ideas of others; they simply wait for the other person to stop speaking so that they may begin. If all ideas are not given serious consideration by all participants in the class, little is gained from a class discussion. There is an old saying that bears repeating: "Keep your ears open; you might learn something."

Presenting Your Ideas

When you have the opportunity to speak in class, present your ideas in a logical order, draw your conclusions, and then stop. You may clarify and illustrate points, but little is gained by simple repetition. Later, if you have other ideas that support your viewpoint, you may express them, following the same guidelines. If you gain the floor just to repeat the points you made previously, you will bore the members of the class, and you will actually hurt your chance of convincing them that you are right.

A Group Effort

Class discussions are excellent ways to learn material. Everyone can share knowledge, and everyone will profit. Prepare properly, listen attentively, and make your points logically. Your opinion will be valued, and you will learn.

17-1 WORK TOGETHER, p. 518

Estimating and journalizing entries for uncollectible accounts expense

1.

Velson Company

Work Sheet

For Year Ended December 31, 20 – –

	ACCOUNT TITLE	TRIAL BALANCE		ADJUSTMENTS	
		DEBIT	CREDIT	DEBIT	CREDIT
6	Accounts Receivable	867 680 00			
7	Allowance for Uncollectible Accounts		8 53 00		
47	Uncollectible Accounts Expense				

2., 3.

GENERAL JOURNAL   PAGE 13

	DATE	ACCOUNT TITLE	DOC. NO.	POST. REF.	DEBIT	CREDIT	
3							3
4							4
5							5

3.   **GENERAL LEDGER**

ACCOUNT Accounts Receivable   ACCOUNT NO. 1130

DATE	ITEM	POST. REF.	DEBIT	CREDIT	BALANCE	
					DEBIT	CREDIT
20 – – Dec. 31	Balance	✔			867 680 00	

ACCOUNT Allowance for Uncollectible Accounts   ACCOUNT NO. 1135

DATE	ITEM	POST. REF.	DEBIT	CREDIT	BALANCE	
					DEBIT	CREDIT
20 – – Dec. 31	Balance	✔				8 53 00

ACCOUNT Uncollectible Accounts Expense   ACCOUNT NO. 6165

DATE	ITEM	POST. REF.	DEBIT	CREDIT	BALANCE	
					DEBIT	CREDIT

Estimating and journalizing entries for uncollectible accounts expense

1.

McCaffery Industries

Work Sheet

For Year Ended December 31, 20 – –

	ACCOUNT TITLE	TRIAL BALANCE DEBIT	TRIAL BALANCE CREDIT	ADJUSTMENTS DEBIT	ADJUSTMENTS CREDIT
6	Accounts Receivable	131 8 4 8 50			
7	Allowance for Uncollectible Accounts		2 1 6 00		
47	Uncollectible Accounts Expense				

2., 3.

GENERAL JOURNAL PAGE 26

	DATE	ACCOUNT TITLE	DOC. NO.	POST. REF.	DEBIT	CREDIT	
3							3
4							4
5							5

3. **GENERAL LEDGER**

ACCOUNT Accounts Receivable   ACCOUNT NO. 1130

DATE	ITEM	POST. REF.	DEBIT	CREDIT	BALANCE DEBIT	BALANCE CREDIT
20 – – Dec. 31	Balance	✔			131 8 4 8 50	

ACCOUNT Allowance for Uncollectible Accounts   ACCOUNT NO. 1135

DATE	ITEM	POST. REF.	DEBIT	CREDIT	BALANCE DEBIT	BALANCE CREDIT
20 – – Dec. 31	Balance	✔				2 1 6 00

ACCOUNT Uncollectible Accounts Expense   ACCOUNT NO. 6165

DATE	ITEM	POST. REF.	DEBIT	CREDIT	BALANCE DEBIT	BALANCE CREDIT

17-2 **WORK TOGETHER, p. 524**

Recording entries related to uncollectible accounts receivable

1., 2., 3.

GENERAL JOURNAL

PAGE 15

DATE	ACCOUNT TITLE	DOC. NO.	POST. REF.	DEBIT	CREDIT

1., 2.

CASH RECEIPTS JOURNAL

PAGE 24

DATE	ACCOUNT TITLE	DOC. NO.	POST. REF.	GENERAL DEBIT	GENERAL CREDIT	ACCOUNTS RECEIVABLE CREDIT	SALES CREDIT	SALES TAX PAYABLE CREDIT	SALES DISCOUNT DEBIT	CASH DEBIT

2.

ACCOUNTS RECEIVABLE LEDGER

CUSTOMER Davidson Corp.   CUSTOMER NO. 110

DATE	ITEM	POST. REF.	DEBIT	CREDIT	DEBIT BALANCE
20-- Jan. 9		S1	8 4 9 00		8 4 9 00

CUSTOMER JGF Industries   CUSTOMER NO. 120

DATE	ITEM	POST. REF.	DEBIT	CREDIT	DEBIT BALANCE
20-- Mar. 13		S4	2 4 8 8 00		2 4 8 8 00

CUSTOMER Lynchburg Co.   CUSTOMER NO. 130

DATE	ITEM	POST. REF.	DEBIT	CREDIT	DEBIT BALANCE
20-- Apr. 23	Written off	G5		1 5 4 8 00	—

CUSTOMER Sansing Co.   CUSTOMER NO. 140

DATE	ITEM	POST. REF.	DEBIT	CREDIT	DEBIT BALANCE
20-- Jan. 22		S2	6 0 9 00		6 0 9 00

17-2 WORK TOGETHER (concluded)

3.

GENERAL LEDGER

ACCOUNT Accounts Receivable ACCOUNT NO. 1125

DATE	ITEM	POST. REF.	DEBIT	CREDIT	BALANCE DEBIT	BALANCE CREDIT
20-- Nov. 1	Balance	✔			50 1 4 8 00	

ACCOUNT Allowance for Uncollectible Accounts ACCOUNT NO. 1130

DATE	ITEM	POST. REF.	DEBIT	CREDIT	BALANCE DEBIT	BALANCE CREDIT
20-- Nov. 1	Balance	✔				4 9 5 8 00

Recording entries related to uncollectible accounts receivable

1., 2., 3.

GENERAL JOURNAL

PAGE 11

	DATE	ACCOUNT TITLE	DOC. NO.	POST. REF.	DEBIT	CREDIT	
1							1
2							2
3							3
4							4
5							5
6							6
7							7
8							8
9							9
10							10
11							11
12							12

1., 2.

CASH RECEIPTS JOURNAL

PAGE 15

	DATE	ACCOUNT TITLE	DOC. NO.	POST. REF.	GENERAL DEBIT	GENERAL CREDIT	ACCOUNTS RECEIVABLE CREDIT	SALES CREDIT	SALES TAX PAYABLE CREDIT	SALES DISCOUNT DEBIT	CASH DEBIT	
1												1
2												2
3												3
4												4
5												5

17-2 ON YOUR OWN (continued)

2.

ACCOUNTS RECEIVABLE LEDGER

CUSTOMER Peter Ewing   CUSTOMER NO. 110

DATE		ITEM	POST. REF.	DEBIT	CREDIT	DEBIT BALANCE
20-- Jan.	9		S1	6 1 2 00		6 1 2 00

CUSTOMER Tim Haley   CUSTOMER NO. 120

DATE		ITEM	POST. REF.	DEBIT	CREDIT	DEBIT BALANCE
20-- Mar.	13		S3	2 3 8 00		2 3 8 00

CUSTOMER Mike Novak   CUSTOMER NO. 130

DATE		ITEM	POST. REF.	DEBIT	CREDIT	DEBIT BALANCE
20-- Apr.	6	Written off	G4		8 5 3 00	—

CUSTOMER Angela White   CUSTOMER NO. 140

DATE		ITEM	POST. REF.	DEBIT	CREDIT	DEBIT BALANCE
20-- Feb.	23		S2	1 5 9 00		1 5 9 00

3.

GENERAL LEDGER

ACCOUNT Accounts Receivable   ACCOUNT NO. 1125

DATE		ITEM	POST. REF.	DEBIT	CREDIT	BALANCE	
						DEBIT	CREDIT
Oct.	1	Balance	✔			50 1 4 8 00	

ACCOUNT Allowance for Uncollectible Accounts   ACCOUNT NO. 1130

DATE		ITEM	POST. REF.	DEBIT	CREDIT	BALANCE	
						DEBIT	CREDIT
Oct.	1	Balance	✔				3 4 5 8 00

17-1 APPLICATION PROBLEM, p. 526

Estimating and journalizing entries for uncollectible accounts expense

1.

Kellogg, Inc.

Work Sheet

For Year Ended December 31, 20 – –

		1	2	3	4
		TRIAL BALANCE		ADJUSTMENTS	
	ACCOUNT TITLE	DEBIT	CREDIT	DEBIT	CREDIT
6	Accounts Receivable	125 84 8 33			
7	Allowance for Uncollectible Accounts		5 3 4 00		
47	Uncollectible Accounts Expense				

2., 3.

GENERAL JOURNAL   PAGE 25

	DATE	ACCOUNT TITLE	DOC. NO.	POST. REF.	DEBIT	CREDIT	
3							3
4							4
5							5

3.   **GENERAL LEDGER**

ACCOUNT Accounts Receivable   ACCOUNT NO. 1125

DATE	ITEM	POST. REF.	DEBIT	CREDIT	BALANCE DEBIT	BALANCE CREDIT
20– – Dec. 31	Balance	✔			125 84 8 33	

ACCOUNT Allowance for Uncollectible Accounts   ACCOUNT NO. 1130

DATE	ITEM	POST. REF.	DEBIT	CREDIT	BALANCE DEBIT	BALANCE CREDIT
20– – Dec. 31	Balance	✔				5 3 4 00

ACCOUNT Uncollectible Accounts Expense   ACCOUNT NO. 6165

DATE	ITEM	POST. REF.	DEBIT	CREDIT	BALANCE DEBIT	BALANCE CREDIT

Recording entries related to uncollectible accounts receivable

1., 2., 3.

GENERAL JOURNAL

PAGE 14

	DATE	ACCOUNT TITLE	DOC. NO.	POST. REF.	DEBIT	CREDIT	
1							1
2							2
3							3
4							4
5							5
6							6
7							7
8							8
9							9
10							10
11							11
12							12

1., 2.

CASH RECEIPTS JOURNAL

PAGE 19

	DATE	ACCOUNT TITLE	DOC. NO.	POST. REF.	GENERAL DEBIT	GENERAL CREDIT	ACCOUNTS RECEIVABLE CREDIT	SALES CREDIT	SALES TAX PAYABLE CREDIT	SALES DISCOUNT DEBIT	CASH DEBIT	
					1	2	3	4	5	6	7	
1												1
2												2
3												3
4												4
5												5

17-2 **APPLICATION PROBLEM (continued)**

2.

ACCOUNTS RECEIVABLE LEDGER

CUSTOMER Davis Industries   CUSTOMER NO. 110

	DATE	ITEM	POST. REF.	DEBIT	CREDIT	DEBIT BALANCE
20-- Feb.	23	Written off	G2		1 8 5 00	—

CUSTOMER Jackson Company   CUSTOMER NO. 120

	DATE	ITEM	POST. REF.	DEBIT	CREDIT	DEBIT BALANCE
20-- Jan.	4		S1	1 2 4 00		1 2 4 00

CUSTOMER Lancing, Inc.   CUSTOMER NO. 130

	DATE	ITEM	POST. REF.	DEBIT	CREDIT	DEBIT BALANCE
20-- Apr.	2		S7	2 1 5 00		2 1 5 00

CUSTOMER Sanders Mfg.   CUSTOMER NO. 140

	DATE	ITEM	POST. REF.	DEBIT	CREDIT	DEBIT BALANCE
20-- Jan.	23		S2	8 4 2 00		8 4 2 00

3.

GENERAL LEDGER

ACCOUNT Accounts Receivable   ACCOUNT NO. 1125

DATE		ITEM	POST. REF.	DEBIT	CREDIT	BALANCE	
						DEBIT	CREDIT
Sept.	1	Balance	✔			23 4 8 4 00	

ACCOUNT Allowance for Uncollectible Accounts   ACCOUNT NO. 1130

DATE		ITEM	POST. REF.	DEBIT	CREDIT	BALANCE	
						DEBIT	CREDIT
Sept.	1	Balance	✔				2 4 4 8 00

17-3 APPLICATION PROBLEM, p. 527

Recording entries related to uncollectible accounts receivable

1., 2., 3.

GENERAL JOURNAL

PAGE 4

	DATE	ACCOUNT TITLE	DOC. NO.	POST. REF.	DEBIT	CREDIT	
1							1
2							2
3							3
4							4
5							5
6							6
7							7
8							8
9							9
10							10
11							11
12							12
13							13
14							14

1., 2.

CASH RECEIPTS JOURNAL

PAGE 2

	DATE	ACCOUNT TITLE	DOC. NO.	POST. REF.	GENERAL DEBIT	GENERAL CREDIT	ACCOUNTS RECEIVABLE CREDIT	SALES CREDIT	SALES TAX PAYABLE CREDIT	SALES DISCOUNT DEBIT	CASH DEBIT	
					1	2	3	4	5	6	7	
1												1
2												2
3												3
4												4
5												5

2.

ACCOUNTS RECEIVABLE LEDGER

CUSTOMER Bearden Co.   CUSTOMER NO. 110

DATE		ITEM	POST. REF.	DEBIT	CREDIT	DEBIT BALANCE
Jan. ²⁰⁻⁻	3	Written off	G1		1 4 5 8 00	—

CUSTOMER Camden Enterprises   CUSTOMER NO. 120

DATE		ITEM	POST. REF.	DEBIT	CREDIT	DEBIT BALANCE
Jan. ²⁰⁻⁻	3	Written off	G1		1 7 8 4 00	—

CUSTOMER Hampton Industries   CUSTOMER NO. 130

DATE		ITEM	POST. REF.	DEBIT	CREDIT	DEBIT BALANCE
Jan. ²⁰⁻⁻	1	Balance	✔			2 5 8 4 00

CUSTOMER Rankin Co.   CUSTOMER NO. 140

DATE		ITEM	POST. REF.	DEBIT	CREDIT	DEBIT BALANCE
Jan. ²⁰⁻⁻	1	Balance	✔			9 4 8 00

CUSTOMER Wilmont Co.   CUSTOMER NO. 150

DATE		ITEM	POST. REF.	DEBIT	CREDIT	DEBIT BALANCE
Jan. ²⁰⁻⁻	1	Balance	✔			5 4 8 00

17-3 **APPLICATION PROBLEM (concluded)**

3.

GENERAL LEDGER

account Accounts Receivable   account no. 1130

DATE		ITEM	POST. REF.	DEBIT	CREDIT	BALANCE	
						DEBIT	CREDIT
Feb.	1	Balance	✔			54 1 5 8 00	

account Allowance for Uncollectible Accounts   account no. 1135

DATE		ITEM	POST. REF.	DEBIT	CREDIT	BALANCE	
						DEBIT	CREDIT
Feb.	1	Balance	✔				2 5 1 4 00

Recording entries for uncollectible accounts

1.

GENERAL JOURNAL   PAGE 20

	DATE	ACCOUNT TITLE	DOC. NO.	POST. REF.	DEBIT	CREDIT	
1							1
2							2
3							3
4							4
5							5

2.

GENERAL JOURNAL   PAGE 22

	DATE	ACCOUNT TITLE	DOC. NO.	POST. REF.	DEBIT	CREDIT	
1							1
2							2
3							3
4							4
5							5
6							6

3.

GENERAL JOURNAL   PAGE 24

	DATE	ACCOUNT TITLE	DOC. NO.	POST. REF.	DEBIT	CREDIT	
1							1
2							2
3							3
4							4
5							5
6							6

4.

GENERAL JOURNAL   PAGE 26

	DATE	ACCOUNT TITLE	DOC. NO.	POST. REF.	DEBIT	CREDIT	
1							1
2							2
3							3
4							4
5							5

17-4 MASTERY PROBLEM (continued)

2.

CASH RECEIPTS JOURNAL

PAGE 24

DATE	ACCOUNT TITLE	DOC. NO.	POST. REF.	GENERAL DEBIT (1)	GENERAL CREDIT (2)	ACCOUNTS RECEIVABLE CREDIT (3)	SALES CREDIT (4)	SALES TAX PAYABLE CREDIT (5)	SALES DISCOUNT DEBIT (6)	CASH DEBIT (7)

3.

CASH RECEIPTS JOURNAL

PAGE 26

DATE	ACCOUNT TITLE	DOC. NO.	POST. REF.	GENERAL DEBIT (1)	GENERAL CREDIT (2)	ACCOUNTS RECEIVABLE CREDIT (3)	SALES CREDIT (4)	SALES TAX PAYABLE CREDIT (5)	SALES DISCOUNT DEBIT (6)	CASH DEBIT (7)

MASTERY PROBLEM (continued)

1., 2., 3.

ACCOUNTS RECEIVABLE LEDGER

CUSTOMER Baker Corp.   CUSTOMER NO. 110

DATE		ITEM	POST. REF.	DEBIT	CREDIT	DEBIT BALANCE
20-- Feb.	11		S4	8 1 5 00		8 1 5 00

CUSTOMER Franklin, Inc.   CUSTOMER NO. 120

DATE		ITEM	POST. REF.	DEBIT	CREDIT	DEBIT BALANCE
20-- Mar.	15		S5	1 4 5 8 00		1 4 5 8 00

CUSTOMER Gason Company   CUSTOMER NO. 130

DATE		ITEM	POST. REF.	DEBIT	CREDIT	DEBIT BALANCE
20-- Jan.	1	Balance	✔			9 4 8 00

CUSTOMER Keller Corporation   CUSTOMER NO. 140

DATE		ITEM	POST. REF.	DEBIT	CREDIT	DEBIT BALANCE
20-- Jan.	1	Balance	✔			6 4 8 25

CUSTOMER Pearson Industries   CUSTOMER NO. 150

DATE		ITEM	POST. REF.	DEBIT	CREDIT	DEBIT BALANCE
20-- Apr.	14	Written off	G8		2 5 1 80	—

17-4 MASTERY PROBLEM (concluded)

1., 2., 3., 4.

GENERAL LEDGER

ACCOUNT Accounts Receivable   ACCOUNT NO. 1125

DATE		ITEM	POST. REF.	DEBIT	CREDIT	BALANCE	
						DEBIT	CREDIT
20-- Oct.	1	Balance	✔			68 45 2 30	

ACCOUNT Allowance for Uncollectible Accounts   ACCOUNT NO. 1130

DATE		ITEM	POST. REF.	DEBIT	CREDIT	BALANCE	
						DEBIT	CREDIT
20-- Oct.	1	Balance	✔				3 2 1 0 00

ACCOUNT Uncollectible Accounts Expense   ACCOUNT NO. 6165

DATE	ITEM	POST. REF.	DEBIT	CREDIT	BALANCE	
					DEBIT	CREDIT

Recording entries for uncollectible accounts

Study Guide 18

Name	Perfect Score	Your Score
Identifying Accounting Terms	7 Pts.	
Analyzing Plant Asset Transactions	14 Pts.	
Analyzing Plant Assets and Depreciation	10 Pts.	
Total	31 Pts.	

Part One—Identifying Accounting Terms

Directions: Select the one term in Column I that best fits each definition in Column II. Print the letter identifying your choice in the Answers column.

Column I	Column II	Answers
A. assessed value	**1.** Land and anything attached to the land. (p. 536)	1. _____
B. declining-balance method of depreciation	**2.** All property not classified as real property. (p. 536)	2. _____
C. gain on plant assets	**3.** The value of an asset determined by tax authorities for the purpose of calculating taxes. (p. 536)	3. _____
D. loss on plant assets	**4.** An accounting form on which a business records information about each plant asset. (p. 542)	4. _____
E. personal property	**5.** Revenue that results when a plant asset is sold for more than book value. (p. 548)	5. _____
F. plant asset record	**6.** The loss that results when a plant asset is sold for less than book value. (p. 549)	6. _____
G. real property	**7.** Multiplying the book value by a constant depreciation rate at the end of each fiscal period. (p. 551)	7. _____

Part Two—Analyzing Plant Asset Transactions

Directions: Analyze each of the following transactions into debit and credit parts. Print the letter identifying your choices in the proper Answers column.

Account Titles	Transactions	Answers Debit	Credit
A. Accumulated Depreciation—Office Equipment	**1–2.** Paid cash for new display case. (p. 535)	1. _____	2. _____
B. Accumulated Depreciation—Store Equipment	**3–4.** Paid cash for property taxes. (p. 536)	3. _____	4. _____
C. Cash	**5–6.** Recorded annual store equipment depreciation. (p. 543)	5. _____	6. _____
D. Depreciation Expense—Office Equipment	**7–8.** Received cash from sale of display case for book value. (p. 546)	7. _____	8. _____
E. Depreciation Expense—Store Equipment	**9–10.** Recorded a partial year's depreciation on a cash register to be sold. (p. 547)	9. _____	10. _____
F. Gain on Plant Assets	**11–12.** Received cash from sale of cash register for more than book value. (p. 548)	11. _____	12. _____
G. Office Equipment	**13–14.** Received cash from sale of a computer for less than book value. (p. 549)	13. _____	14. _____
H. Loss on Plant Assets			
I. Property Tax Expense			
J. Store Equipment			

Part Three—Analyzing Plant Assets and Depreciation

Directions: For each of the following items, select the choice that best completes the statement. Print the letter identifying your choice in the Answers column.

Answers

1. Recording a plant asset at its original cost is an application of the concept (A) Going Concern (B) Matching Expenses with Revenue (C) Objective Evidence (D) Historical Cost (p. 535)

1. _____

2. The smallest unit of time used to calculate depreciation is (A) one month (B) half a year (C) one year (D) none of these (p. 539)

2. _____

3. The annual depreciation for a plant asset with original cost of $1,000.00, estimated salvage value of $100.00, and estimated useful life of 10 years, using the straight-line method, is (A) $100.00 (B) $1,000.00 (C) $900.00 (D) $90.00 (p. 539)

3. _____

4. The accumulated depreciation account should show (A) total depreciation for plant assets since the business was formed (B) total depreciation for plant assets still in use (C) only total depreciation expense for plant assets for the current year (D) next year's estimated depreciation for plant assets (p. 540)

4. _____

5. When a plant asset is sold for the asset's book value, (A) cash received plus accumulated depreciation equals original cost (B) cash received plus salvage value equals original cost (C) cash received plus accumulated depreciation plus salvage value equals original cost (D) none of these (p. 546)

5. _____

6. When a plant asset is sold for more than the asset's book value, (A) cash received plus accumulated depreciation plus gain on disposal equals original cost plus gain on disposal (B) cash received plus accumulated depreciation equals original cost plus gain on disposal (C) cash received plus accumulated depreciation plus loss on disposal equals original cost (D) cash received plus accumulated depreciation equals original cost plus loss on disposal (p. 548)

6. _____

7. When a plant asset is sold for less than the asset's book value, (A) cash received plus accumulated depreciation plus gain on disposal equals original cost (B) cash received plus accumulated depreciation plus loss on disposal equals original cost (C) cash received plus accumulated depreciation equals original cost plus gain on disposal (D) cash received plus accumulated depreciation equals original cost plus loss on disposal (p. 549)

7. _____

8. Charging more depreciation expense in the early years is an application of the concept of (A) Matching Expenses with Revenue (B) Realization of Revenue (C) Adequate Disclosure (D) Historical Cost (p. 551)

8. _____

9. The declining-balance method of depreciation is calculated by (A) charging an equal amount of depreciation each year (B) subtracting the annual depreciation expense from the book value (C) multiplying the book value by a constant depreciation rate at the end of each fiscal period (D) none of the above (p. 551)

9. _____

10. The double declining-balance method of depreciation (A) records a greater depreciation expense in the early years of an asset's useful life (B) records a lesser depreciation expense in the early years of an asset's useful life (C) slows down the recording of depreciation in the early years of an asset's useful life (D) accelerates the recording of depreciation in the later years of an asset's useful life (p. 553)

10. _____

18-1 WORK TOGETHER, p. 537

Journalizing buying plant assets and paying property tax

1., 2.

CASH PAYMENTS JOURNAL

PAGE 1

				1	2	3	4	5
				GENERAL		ACCOUNTS PAYABLE DEBIT	PURCHASES DISCOUNT CREDIT	CASH CREDIT
DATE	ACCOUNT TITLE	CK. NO.	POST. REF.	DEBIT	CREDIT			
									1
									2
									3
									4

GENERAL LEDGER

2.

ACCOUNT Office Equipment   ACCOUNT NO. 1205

DATE	ITEM	POST. REF.	DEBIT	CREDIT	BALANCE DEBIT	BALANCE CREDIT
20-- Jan. 1	Balance	✓			15 4 8 0 00	

ACCOUNT Store Equipment   ACCOUNT NO. 1215

DATE	ITEM	POST. REF.	DEBIT	CREDIT	BALANCE DEBIT	BALANCE CREDIT
20-- Jan. 1	Balance	✓			9 7 3 0 00	

ACCOUNT Property Tax Expense   ACCOUNT NO. 6145

DATE	ITEM	POST. REF.	DEBIT	CREDIT	BALANCE DEBIT	BALANCE CREDIT

Journalizing buying plant assets and paying property tax

1., 2.

CASH PAYMENTS JOURNAL

PAGE 1

					1 GENERAL		2	3 ACCOUNTS PAYABLE DEBIT	4 PURCHASES DISCOUNT CREDIT	5 CASH CREDIT	
DATE	ACCOUNT TITLE	CK. NO.	POST. REF.		DEBIT	CREDIT					
											1
											2
											3
											4

2.

GENERAL LEDGER

ACCOUNT Office Equipment   ACCOUNT NO. 1205

DATE	ITEM	POST. REF.	DEBIT	CREDIT	BALANCE DEBIT	BALANCE CREDIT
20-- Jan. 1	Balance	✓			1548000	

ACCOUNT Store Equipment   ACCOUNT NO. 1215

DATE	ITEM	POST. REF.	DEBIT	CREDIT	BALANCE DEBIT	BALANCE CREDIT
20-- Jan. 1	Balance	✓			973000	

ACCOUNT Property Tax Expense   ACCOUNT NO. 6145

DATE	ITEM	POST. REF.	DEBIT	CREDIT	BALANCE DEBIT	BALANCE CREDIT

18-2 WORK TOGETHER, p. 541

Calculating depreciation

Plant asset:	_____	Original cost:	_____
Depreciation method:	_____	Estimated salvage value:	_____
		Estimated useful life:	_____
		Date bought:	_____

Year	Beginning Book Value	Annual Depreciation	Accumulated Depreciation	Ending Book Value

Plant asset:	_____	Original cost:	_____
Depreciation method:	_____	Estimated salvage value:	_____
		Estimated useful life:	_____
		Date bought:	_____

Year	Beginning Book Value	Annual Depreciation	Accumulated Depreciation	Ending Book Value

Calculating depreciation

Plant asset:		Original cost:		
Depreciation method:		Estimated salvage value:		
		Estimated useful life:		
		Date bought:		

Year	Beginning Book Value	Annual Depreciation	Accumulated Depreciation	Ending Book Value

Plant asset:		Original cost:		
Depreciation method:		Estimated salvage value:		
		Estimated useful life:		
		Date bought:		

Year	Beginning Book Value	Annual Depreciation	Accumulated Depreciation	Ending Book Value

Name _____ Date _____ Class _____

18-3 WORK TOGETHER, p. 545

Journalizing depreciation

1.

| PLANT ASSET RECORD No. ____ | | General Ledger Account No. _____ |

Description _____   General Ledger Account _____

Date   Serial
Bought _____ Number _____   Original Cost _____

                        Estimated
Estimated   Salvage   Depreciation
Useful Life _____ Value _____   Method _____

Disposed of: Discarded _____   Sold _____   Traded _____
Date _____   Disposal Amount _____

Year	Annual Depreciation Expense	Accumulated Depreciation	Ending Book Value

| PLANT ASSET RECORD No. ____ | | General Ledger Account No. _____ |

Description _____   General Ledger Account _____

Date   Serial
Bought _____ Number _____   Original Cost _____

                        Estimated
Estimated   Salvage   Depreciation
Useful Life _____ Value _____   Method _____

Disposed of: Discarded _____   Sold _____   Traded _____
Date _____   Disposal Amount _____

Year	Annual Depreciation Expense	Accumulated Depreciation	Ending Book Value

2.

Fairbrother, Inc.

Work Sheet

For Year Ended December 31, 20 – –

	ACCOUNT TITLE	TRIAL BALANCE DEBIT	TRIAL BALANCE CREDIT	ADJUSTMENTS DEBIT	ADJUSTMENTS CREDIT
10	Office Equipment	28 4 8 5 25			
11	Accumulated Depreciation—Office Equipment		14 5 2 2 00		
38	Depreciation Expense—Office Equipment				

GENERAL JOURNAL   PAGE 20

	DATE	ACCOUNT TITLE	DOC. NO.	POST. REF.	DEBIT	CREDIT	
1							1
2							2
3							3
4							4
5							5

GENERAL LEDGER

ACCOUNT Office Equipment   ACCOUNT NO. 1205

DATE	ITEM	POST. REF.	DEBIT	CREDIT	BALANCE DEBIT	BALANCE CREDIT
20-- Dec. 31	Balance	✔			28 4 8 5 25	

ACCOUNT Accumulated Depreciation—Office Equipment   ACCOUNT NO. 1210

DATE	ITEM	POST. REF.	DEBIT	CREDIT	BALANCE DEBIT	BALANCE CREDIT
20-- Dec. 31	Balance	✔				14 5 2 2 00

ACCOUNT Depreciation Expense—Office Equipment   ACCOUNT NO. 6120

DATE	ITEM	POST. REF.	DEBIT	CREDIT	BALANCE DEBIT	BALANCE CREDIT

18-3 ON YOUR OWN, p. 545

Journalizing depreciation

1.

PLANT ASSET RECORD No. ____   General Ledger Account No. _____

Description _____   General Ledger Account _____

Date   Serial
Bought _____   Number _____   Original Cost _____

                              Estimated
Estimated   Salvage   Depreciation
Useful Life _____   Value _____   Method _____

Disposed of: Discarded _____   Sold _____   Traded _____
Date _____   Disposal Amount _____

Year	Annual Depreciation Expense	Accumulated Depreciation	Ending Book Value

PLANT ASSET RECORD No. ____   General Ledger Account No. _____

Description _____   General Ledger Account _____

Date   Serial
Bought _____   Number _____   Original Cost _____

                              Estimated
Estimated   Salvage   Depreciation
Useful Life _____   Value _____   Method _____

Disposed of: Discarded _____   Sold _____   Traded _____
Date _____   Disposal Amount _____

Year	Annual Depreciation Expense	Accumulated Depreciation	Ending Book Value

ON YOUR OWN (concluded)

2.

Wrench Co.

Work Sheet

For Year Ended December 31, 20 – –

			1	2	3	4
	ACCOUNT TITLE		TRIAL BALANCE		ADJUSTMENTS	
			DEBIT	CREDIT	DEBIT	CREDIT
12	Store Equipment		35 8 4 8 22			
13	Accumulated Depreciation—Store Equipment			24 1 1 8 00		
39	Depreciation Expense—Store Equipment					

GENERAL JOURNAL

PAGE 18

	DATE	ACCOUNT TITLE	DOC. NO.	POST. REF.	DEBIT	CREDIT	
1							1
2							2
3							3
4							4

GENERAL LEDGER

ACCOUNT Store Equipment   ACCOUNT NO. 1215

DATE	ITEM	POST. REF.	DEBIT	CREDIT	BALANCE DEBIT	BALANCE CREDIT
20 – – Dec. 31	Balance	✔			35 8 4 8 22	

ACCOUNT Accumulated Depreciation—Store Equipment   ACCOUNT NO. 1220

DATE	ITEM	POST. REF.	DEBIT	CREDIT	BALANCE DEBIT	BALANCE CREDIT
20 – – Dec. 31	Balance	✔				24 1 1 8 00

ACCOUNT Depreciation Expense—Store Equipment   ACCOUNT NO. 6125

DATE	ITEM	POST. REF.	DEBIT	CREDIT	BALANCE DEBIT	BALANCE CREDIT

18-4 WORK TOGETHER, p. 550

Recording the disposal of plant assets

1.

GENERAL JOURNAL   PAGE 11

	DATE	ACCOUNT TITLE	DOC. NO.	POST. REF.	DEBIT	CREDIT	
1							1
2							2
3							3
4							4
5							5

2.

CASH RECEIPTS JOURNAL   PAGE 1

	DATE	ACCOUNT TITLE	DOC. NO.	POST. REF.	GENERAL DEBIT	GENERAL CREDIT	ACCOUNTS RECEIVABLE CREDIT	SALES CREDIT	SALES TAX PAYABLE CREDIT	SALES DISCOUNT DEBIT	CASH DEBIT	
1												1
2												2
3												3
4												4
5												5
6												6
7												7

Recording the disposal of plant assets

1.

GENERAL JOURNAL

PAGE 10

	DATE	ACCOUNT TITLE	DOC. NO.	POST. REF.	DEBIT	CREDIT	
1							1
2							2
3							3
4							4
5							5

2.

CASH RECEIPTS JOURNAL

PAGE 8

	DATE	ACCOUNT TITLE	DOC. NO.	POST. REF.	GENERAL DEBIT	GENERAL CREDIT	ACCOUNTS RECEIVABLE CREDIT	SALES CREDIT	SALES TAX PAYABLE CREDIT	SALES DISCOUNT DEBIT	CASH DEBIT	
1												1
2												2
3												3
4												4
5												5
6												6

18-5 WORK TOGETHER, p. 554

Calculating depreciation using the double declining-balance depreciation method

Plant asset: _____   Original cost: _____
Depreciation method: _____   Estimated salvage value: _____
                                              Estimated useful life: _____

Year	Beginning Book Value	Declining-Balance Rate	Annual Depreciation	Ending Book Value

Plant asset: _____   Original cost: _____
Depreciation method: _____   Estimated salvage value: _____
                                              Estimated useful life: _____

Year	Beginning Book Value	Declining-Balance Rate	Annual Depreciation	Ending Book Value

Plant asset: _____   Original cost: _____
Depreciation method: _____   Estimated salvage value: _____
                                              Estimated useful life: _____

Year	Beginning Book Value	Declining-Balance Rate	Annual Depreciation	Ending Book Value

Calculating depreciation using the double declining-balance depreciation method

Plant asset: _____ Original cost: _____

Depreciation method: _____ Estimated salvage value _____

Estimated useful life: _____

Year	Beginning Book Value	Declining-Balance Rate	Annual Depreciation	Ending Book Value

Plant asset: _____ Original cost: _____

Depreciation method: _____ Estimated salvage value: _____

Estimated useful life: _____

Year	Beginning Book Value	Declining-Balance Rate	Annual Depreciation	Ending Book Value

Plant asset: _____ Original cost: _____

Depreciation method: _____ Estimated salvage value: _____

Estimated useful life _____

Year	Beginning Book Value	Declining-Balance Rate	Annual Depreciation	Ending Book Value

18-1 APPLICATION PROBLEM, p. 556

Journalizing buying plant assets and paying property tax

1., 2.

CASH PAYMENTS JOURNAL

PAGE 1

					1 GENERAL		3 ACCOUNTS PAYABLE DEBIT	4 PURCHASES DISCOUNT CREDIT	5 CASH CREDIT
DATE	ACCOUNT TITLE	CK. NO.	POST. REF.		DEBIT	CREDIT			
1									
2									
3									
4									
5									

2.

GENERAL LEDGER

ACCOUNT Office Equipment   ACCOUNT NO. 1205

DATE	ITEM	POST. REF.	DEBIT	CREDIT	BALANCE DEBIT	BALANCE CREDIT
20-- Jan. 1	Balance	✓			15 8 4 8 50	

ACCOUNT Store Equipment   ACCOUNT NO. 1215

DATE	ITEM	POST. REF.	DEBIT	CREDIT	BALANCE DEBIT	BALANCE CREDIT
20-- Jan. 1	Balance	✓			82 4 8 3 75	

ACCOUNT Property Tax Expense   ACCOUNT NO. 6145

DATE	ITEM	POST. REF.	DEBIT	CREDIT	BALANCE DEBIT	BALANCE CREDIT

Calculating straight-line depreciation

Plant asset: _____   Original cost: _____
Depreciation method: _____   Estimated salvage value: _____
                                    Estimated useful life: _____

Year	Beginning Book Value	Annual Depreciation	Accumulated Depreciation	Ending Book Value

Plant asset: _____   Original cost: _____
Depreciation method: _____   Estimated salvage value: _____
                                    Estimated useful life: _____

Year	Beginning Book Value	Annual Depreciation	Accumulated Depreciation	Ending Book Value

Plant asset: _____   Original cost: _____
Depreciation method: _____   Estimated salvage value: _____
                                    Estimated useful life: _____

Year	Beginning Book Value	Annual Depreciation	Accumulated Depreciation	Ending Book Value

18-3 APPLICATION PROBLEM, p. 556

Preparing plant asset records

These plant asset records are needed to complete Application Problem 18-5.

PLANT ASSET RECORD No. 311	General Ledger Account No. 1215

Description _____   General Ledger Account Store Equipment

Date Bought _____	Serial Number _____	Original Cost _____

Estimated Useful Life _____	Estimated Salvage Value _____	Depreciation Method _____

Disposed of: Discarded _____ Sold _____ Traded _____

Date _____ Disposal Amount _____

Year	Annual Depreciation Expense	Accumulated Depreciation	Ending Book Value

Continue record on back of card

PLANT ASSET RECORD No. 312   General Ledger Account No. 1205

Description _____   General Ledger Account Office Equipment

Date   Serial
Bought _____   Number _____   Original Cost _____

                             Estimated
Estimated   Salvage   Depreciation
Useful Life _____   Value _____   Method _____

Disposed of: Discarded _____   Sold _____   Traded _____
Date _____   Disposal Amount _____

Year	Annual Depreciation Expense	Accumulated Depreciation	Ending Book Value

Continue record on back of card

18-3 APPLICATION PROBLEM (concluded)

PLANT ASSET RECORD No. 313   General Ledger Account No. 1215

Description _____   General Ledger Account Store Equipment

Date   Serial
Bought _____   Number _____   Original Cost _____

                          Estimated
Estimated   Salvage   Depreciation
Useful Life _____ Value _____   Method _____

Disposed of: Discarded _____ Sold _____ Traded _____
Date _____   Disposal Amount _____

Year	Annual Depreciation Expense	Accumulated Depreciation	Ending Book Value

Continue record on back of card

Journalizing annual depreciation expense

Ester Engineering, Inc.

Work Sheet

For Year Ended December 31, 20 – –

	ACCOUNT TITLE	TRIAL BALANCE		ADJUSTMENTS	
		1 DEBIT	2 CREDIT	3 DEBIT	4 CREDIT
10	Office Equipment	51 2 4 8 25			
11	Accumulated Depreciation—Office Equipment		31 0 0 5 00		
38	Depreciation Expense—Office Equipment				

GENERAL LEDGER

ACCOUNT Office Equipment   ACCOUNT NO. 1205

DATE	ITEM	POST. REF.	DEBIT	CREDIT	BALANCE DEBIT	BALANCE CREDIT
20– – Dec. 31	Balance	✔			51 2 4 8 25	

ACCOUNT Accumulated Depreciation—Office Equipment   ACCOUNT NO. 1210

DATE	ITEM	POST. REF.	DEBIT	CREDIT	BALANCE DEBIT	BALANCE CREDIT
20– – Dec. 31	Balance	✔				31 0 0 5 00

ACCOUNT Depreciation Expense—Office Equipment   ACCOUNT NO. 6120

DATE	ITEM	POST. REF.	DEBIT	CREDIT	BALANCE DEBIT	BALANCE CREDIT

18-4 APPLICATION PROBLEM (concluded)

GENERAL JOURNAL

	DATE	ACCOUNT TITLE	DOC. NO.	POST. REF.	DEBIT	CREDIT	
1							1
2							2
3							3
4							4
5							5

Recording the disposal of plant assets

1.

GENERAL JOURNAL

PAGE 3

DATE	ACCOUNT TITLE	DOC. NO.	POST. REF.	DEBIT	CREDIT	
						1
						2
						3
						4
						5

2.

CASH RECEIPTS JOURNAL

PAGE 3

					1 GENERAL	2 GENERAL	3 ACCOUNTS RECEIVABLE CREDIT	4 SALES CREDIT	5 SALES TAX PAYABLE CREDIT	6 SALES DISCOUNT DEBIT	7 CASH DEBIT	
DATE	ACCOUNT TITLE	DOC. NO.	POST. REF.		DEBIT	CREDIT						
												1
												2
												3
												4
												5
												6
												7
												8
												9
												10
												11
												12
												13

18-6 APPLICATION PROBLEM, p. 557

Calculating depreciation using the double declining-balance depreciation method

Plant asset: _____ Original cost: _____
Depreciation method: _____ Estimated salvage value: _____
                                         Estimated useful life: _____

Year	Beginning Book Value	Declining-Balance Rate	Annual Depreciation	Ending Book Value

Plant asset: _____ Original cost: _____
Depreciation method: _____ Estimated salvage value: _____
                                         Estimated useful life: _____

Year	Beginning Book Value	Declining-Balance Rate	Annual Depreciation	Ending Book Value

Plant asset: _____ Original cost: _____
Depreciation method: _____ Estimated salvage value: _____
                                         Estimated useful life: _____

Year	Beginning Book Value	Declining-Balance Rate	Annual Depreciation	Ending Book Value

Recording transactions for plant assets

1.

CASH PAYMENTS JOURNAL

PAGE 1

| | | | | GENERAL | | ACCOUNTS PAYABLE DEBIT | PURCHASES DISCOUNT CREDIT | CASH CREDIT | |
DATE	ACCOUNT TITLE	CK. NO.	POST. REF.	DEBIT	CREDIT				
									1
									2
									3
									4
									5
									6

18-7 MASTERY PROBLEM (continued)

2., 4., 6.

PLANT ASSET RECORD No. _____   General Ledger Account No. _____

Description _____   General Ledger Account _____

Date   Serial

Bought _____   Number _____   Original Cost _____

              Estimated

Estimated   Salvage   Depreciation

Useful Life _____   Value _____   Method _____

Disposed of: Discarded _____   Sold _____   Traded _____

Date _____   Disposal Amount _____

Year	Annual Depreciation Expense	Accumulated Depreciation	Ending Book Value

PLANT ASSET RECORD No. _____   General Ledger Account No. _____

Description _____   General Ledger Account _____

Date   Serial

Bought _____   Number _____   Original Cost _____

              Estimated

Estimated   Salvage   Depreciation

Useful Life _____   Value _____   Method _____

Disposed of: Discarded _____   Sold _____   Traded _____

Date _____   Disposal Amount _____

Year	Annual Depreciation Expense	Accumulated Depreciation	Ending Book Value

3.

Plant asset:		Original cost:	
Depreciation method:		Estimated salvage value:	
		Estimated useful life:	

Year	Beginning Book Value	Declining-Balance Rate	Annual Depreciation	Ending Book Value

Plant asset:		Original cost:	
Depreciation method:		Estimated salvage value:	
		Estimated useful life:	

Year	Beginning Book Value	Annual Depreciation	Accumulated Depreciation	Ending Book Value

18-7   MASTERY PROBLEM (concluded)

CASH RECEIPTS JOURNAL

PAGE 2

				GENERAL		ACCOUNTS RECEIVABLE CREDIT	SALES CREDIT	SALES TAX PAYABLE CREDIT	SALES DISCOUNT DEBIT	CASH DEBIT
DATE	ACCOUNT TITLE	DOC. NO.	POST. REF.	DEBIT	CREDIT					
			1		2	3	4	5	6	7
1										
2										
3										
4										
5										
6										

5.

GENERAL JOURNAL

PAGE 18

DATE	ACCOUNT TITLE	DOC. NO.	POST. REF.	DEBIT	CREDIT
				1	2
1					
2					
3					
4					
5					

Calculating a partial year's depreciation using the double declining-balance method

Plant asset:	_Lift_	Original cost:	**$3,600.00**
Depreciation method:	_Double declining-balance_	Estimated salvage value:	**$ 250.00**
		Estimated useful life:	**5 years**

Year	Beginning Book Value	Declining-Balance Rate	Annual Depreciation	Ending Book Value

Plant asset:	_Lawnmower_	Original cost:	**$5,400.00**
Depreciation method:	_Double declining-balance_	Estimated salvage value:	**$ 300.00**
		Estimated useful life:	**4 years**

Year	Beginning Book Value	Declining-Balance Rate	Annual Depreciation	Ending Book Value

Study Guide 19

Name	Perfect Score	Your Score
Identifying Accounting Terms	9 Pts.	
Analyzing Inventory Systems	10 Pts.	
Analyzing Lifo, Fifo, and Weighted-Average Methods	12 Pts.	
Total	31 Pts.	

Part One—Identifying Accounting Terms

Directions: Select the one term in Column I that best fits each definition in Column II. Print the letter identifying your choice in the Answers column.

Column I	Column II	Answers
A. first-in, first-out inventory costing method	**1.** A merchandise inventory determined by counting, weighing, or measuring items of merchandise on hand. (p. 565)	1. _____
B. gross profit method of estimating inventory	**2.** A merchandise inventory determined by keeping a continuous record of increases, decreases, and balance on hand. (p. 565)	2. _____
C. inventory record	**3.** A form used during a periodic inventory to record information about each item of merchandise on hand. (p. 566)	3. _____
D. last-in, first-out inventory costing method	**4.** A form used to show the kind of merchandise, quantity received, quantity sold, and balance on hand. (p. 567)	4. _____
E. periodic inventory	**5.** A file of stock records for all merchandise on hand. (p. 567)	5. _____
F. perpetual inventory	**6.** Using the price of merchandise purchased first to calculate the cost of merchandise sold first. (p. 569)	6. _____
G. stock ledger	**7.** Using the price of merchandise purchased last to calculate the cost of merchandise sold first. (p. 570)	7. _____
H. stock record	**8.** Using the average cost of beginning inventory plus merchandise purchased during a fiscal period to calculate the cost of merchandise sold. (p. 571)	8. _____
I. weighted-average inventory costing method	**9.** Estimating inventory by using the previous year's percentage of gross profit on operations. (p. 574)	9. _____

Part Two—Analyzing Inventory Systems

Directions: Place a *T* for True or an *F* for False in the Answers column to
show whether each of the following statements is true or false.

Answers

1. Merchandise inventory on hand is typically the largest current asset of a merchandising business. (p. 564)

1. _____

2. The only financial statement on which the value of merchandise on hand is reported is the income statement. (p. 564)

2. _____

3. Net income of a business can be decreased by maintaining a merchandise inventory that is larger than needed. (p. 565)

3. _____

4. A perpetual inventory is sometimes known as a physical inventory. (p. 565)

4. _____

5. A minimum inventory balance is the amount of merchandise that will typically last until ordered merchandise can be received from vendors. (p. 565)

5. _____

6. A perpetual inventory system provides day-to-day information about the quality of merchandise on hand. (p. 567)

6. _____

7. A periodic inventory should be taken at least once a month, even when perpetual inventory records are kept. (p. 567)

7. _____

8. Some cash registers use optical scanners to read the UPC codes marked on products. (p. 567)

8. _____

9. First-in, first-out is a method used to determine the quantity of each type of merchandise on hand. (p. 569)

9. _____

10. The gross profit method makes it possible to prepare monthly income statements without taking a periodic inventory. (p. 574)

10. _____

Part Three—Analyzing Lifo, Fifo, and Weighted-Average Methods

Directions: For each of the following items, select the choice that best completes the statement. Print the letter identifying your choice in the Answers column.

Answers

1. Calculating an accurate inventory cost to assure that gross profit and net income are reported correctly on the income statement is an application of the accounting concept (A) Consistent Reporting (B) Perpetual Inventory (C) Adequate Disclosure (D) none of these (p. 564)

1. _____

2. When the fifo method is used, cost of merchandise sold is valued at the (A) average price (B) most recent price (C) earliest price (D) none of these (p. 569)

2. _____

3. The fifo method is based on the assumption that the merchandise purchased first is the merchandise (A) sold first (B) sold last (C) in beginning inventory (D) none of these (p. 569)

3. _____

4. When the fifo method is used, ending inventory units are priced at the (A) average price (B) earliest price (C) most recent price (D) none of these (p. 569)

4. _____

5. Using an inventory costing method that charges the most recent costs of merchandise against current revenue is an application of the accounting concept (A) Adequate Disclosure (B) Consistent Reporting (C) Matching Expenses with Revenue (D) none of these (p. 570)

5. _____

6. The lifo method is based on the assumption that the merchandise purchased last is the merchandise (A) sold first (B) sold last (C) in ending inventory (D) none of these (p. 570)

6. _____

7. When the lifo method is used, cost of merchandise sold is priced at the (A) average price (B) earliest price (C) most recent price (D) none of these (p. 570)

7. _____

8. The weighted-average method is based on the assumption that the cost of merchandise sold should be calculated using the (A) average price per unit of beginning inventory (B) average price of ending inventory (C) average price of beginning inventory plus purchases during the fiscal period (D) average price of ending inventory plus purchases during the fiscal period (p. 571)

8. _____

9. When the weighted-average method is used, ending inventory units are priced at the (A) earliest price (B) most recent price (C) average price (D) none of these (p. 571)

9. _____

10. A business that uses the same inventory costing method for all fiscal periods is applying the accounting concept (A) Consistent Reporting (B) Accounting Period Cycle (C) Perpetual Inventory (D) Adequate Disclosure (p. 572)

10. _____

11. In a year of rising prices, the inventory method that gives the lowest possible value for ending inventory is (A) fifo (B) lifo (C) weighted-average (D) gross profit (p. 572)

11. _____

12. In a year of falling prices, the inventory method that gives the lowest possible value for ending inventory is (A) weighted-average (B) lifo (C) fifo (D) gross profit (p. 572)

12. _____

Study Skills

Using the Library

Being able to use the library properly is an invaluable skill for anyone. You should visit the library in your school or community often and take as much time as necessary to become thoroughly familiar with every section.

Never be afraid to ask for help. Any librarian should be happy to help you locate any information that you need. If you don't know where to look for information, ask someone to help you. If you can't find information, ask for assistance. If you don't know how to use special equipment, ask for a demonstration.

The Catalog System
Most libraries use either the Library of Congress System or the Dewey Decimal System. Determine which system your library uses and obtain a floor plan of the library to determine where each section is housed. A floor plan is usually available at the main circulation desk, at each entrance to the building, and near the stairs. Take some time to become familiar with every area; it will save you time later when you want to locate a book.

Texts
If you are preparing to write a paper in a particular subject area, you should become familiar with the texts in that field. You may be able to find a number of books on your topic located in one section of the library.

Reference Books
Your library probably has many types of reference books. In the reference section of your library, you will find such books as atlases, encyclopedias, dictionaries, and various other sources of information. In reference books, you will be able to find information on people, places, and events that you may need for your paper.

Periodicals
You will often want to obtain current information on a subject—information that is less than a year old. Current information may be found in the latest issues of periodicals. Your library probably has a collection of newspapers, magazines, and professional journals that you can use when you need current references.

In addition to the latest issues, you may want to read old newspaper and journal articles. Sometimes the library has actual copies of old papers and journals, and sometimes information is available on microfilm.

Electronic Sources
Your library also subscribes to databases which contain vast amounts of information that is available through a computer terminal. The database may be located in another city or another area of the country; however, you will be able to locate information quickly and easily using a computer. You can even obtain a printed copy by using a printer at your computer terminal.

Make the Most of Your Library
The information in the library is usually available to anyone who wants to use it. The library is a vast source of information and enjoyment. Use it often and well.

19-1 WORK TOGETHER, p. 568

Preparing a stock record

1.

STOCK RECORD

Description 16-Gauge Speaker Wire   Stock No. W-394

Reorder 750   Minimum 300   Location Bin T37

1	2	3	4	5	6	7
INCREASES			DECREASES			BALANCE
DATE	PURCHASE INVOICE NO.	QUANTITY	DATE	SALES INVOICE NO.	QUANTITY	QUANTITY
			Sept. 15	2490	150	400

19-1 ON YOUR OWN, p. 568

Preparing a stock record

1.

STOCK RECORD

Description 8" x 10" white metal frame   Stock No. M-253

Reorder 50   Minimum 20   Location Bin F45

1	2	3	4	5	6	7
INCREASES			DECREASES			BALANCE
DATE	PURCHASE INVOICE NO.	QUANTITY	DATE	SALES INVOICE NO.	QUANTITY	QUANTITY
			Oct. 30	543	20	45

Determining the cost of inventory using the fifo, lifo, and weighted-average inventory costing methods

1.

FIFO Method

Purchase Dates	Units Purchased	Unit Price	Total Cost	FIFO Units on Hand	FIFO Cost
January 1, beginning inventory	14	$30.00	$ 420.00		
March 29, purchases	9	32.00	288.00		
May 6, purchases	10	34.00	340.00		
August 28, purchases	8	36.00	288.00		
November 8, purchases	9	38.00	342.00		
Totals	50		$1,678.00		

LIFO Method

Purchase Dates	Units Purchased	Unit Price	Total Cost	LIFO Units on Hand	LIFO Cost
January 1, beginning inventory	14	$30.00	$ 420.00		
March 29, purchases	9	32.00	288.00		
May 6, purchases	10	34.00	340.00		
August 28, purchases	8	36.00	288.00		
November 8, purchases	9	38.00	342.00		
Totals	50		$1,678.00		

Weighted-Average Method

Purchases Date	Units	Unit Price	Total Cost
January 1, beginning inventory	14	$30.00	
March 29, purchases	9	32.00	
May 6, purchases	10	34.00	
August 28, purchases	8	36.00	
November 8, purchases	9	38.00	
Totals	50		

19-2 ON YOUR OWN, p. 573

Determining the cost of inventory using the fifo, lifo, and weighted-average inventory costing methods

1.

FIFO Method

Purchase Dates	Units Purchased	Unit Price	Total Cost	FIFO Units on Hand	FIFO Cost
January 1, beginning inventory	18	$4.60	$ 82.80		
April 9, purchases	12	4.70	56.40		
June 12, purchases	14	4.80	67.20		
September 22, purchases	15	5.00	75.00		
November 20, purchases	16	5.10	81.60		
Totals	75		$363.00		

LIFO Method

Purchase Dates	Units Purchased	Unit Price	Total Cost	LIFO Units on Hand	LIFO Cost
January 1, beginning inventory	18	$4.60	$ 82.80		
April 9, purchases	12	4.70	56.40		
June 12, purchases	14	4.80	67.20		
September 22, purchases	15	5.00	75.00		
November 20, purchases	16	5.10	81.60		
Totals	75		$363.00		

Weighted-Average Method

Purchases			Total Cost
Date	Units	Unit Price	
January 1, beginning inventory	18	$4.60	
April 9, purchases	12	4.70	
June 12, purchases	14	4.80	
September 22, purchases	15	5.00	
November 20, purchases	16	5.10	
Totals	75		

Estimating ending inventory using the gross profit method

1.

STEP 1

Beginning inventory, June 1 . . . . _____

  Plus net purchases for June 1 to June 30 . . . . _____

  Equals cost of merchandise available for sale . . . . _____

STEP 2

Net sales for June 1 to June 30 . . . . _____

  Times previous year's gross profit percentage . . . . _____

  Equals estimated gross profit on operations . . . . _____

STEP 3

Net sales for June 1 to June 30 . . . . _____

  Less estimated gross profit on operations . . . . _____

  Equals estimated cost of merchandise sold . . . . _____

STEP 4

Cost of merchandise available for sale . . . . _____

  Less estimated cost of merchandise sold . . . . _____

  Equals estimated ending merchandise inventory . . . . _____

2.

Evans Company			
Income Statement			
For Month Ended June 30, 20 – –			
			% OF NET SALES
Operating Revenue:			
Net Sales			
Cost of Merchandise Sold:			
Estimated Beginning Inventory, June 1			
Net Purchases			
Merchandise Available for Sale			
Less Estimated Ending Inventory, June 30			
Cost of Merchandise Sold			
Gross Profit on Operations			
Operating Expenses			
Net Income			

19-3 ON YOUR OWN, p. 576

Estimating ending inventory using the gross profit method

1.

STEP 1

Beginning inventory, April 1 . . . .   _____

Plus net purchases for April 1 to April 30 . . . .   _____

Equals cost of merchandise available for sale . . . .   _____

STEP 2

Net sales for April 1 to April 30 . . . .   _____

Times previous year's gross profit percentage . . . .   _____

Equals estimated gross profit on operations . . . .   _____

STEP 3

Net sales for April 1 to April 30 . . . .   _____

Less estimated gross profit on operations . . . .   _____

Equals estimated cost of merchandise sold . . . .   _____

STEP 4

Cost of merchandise available for sale . . . .   _____

Less estimated cost of merchandise sold . . . .   _____

Equals estimated ending merchandise inventory . . . .   _____

2.

Luke Enterprises					
Income Statement					
For Month Ended April 30, 20 – –					
					% OF NET SALES
Operating Revenue:					
Net Sales					
Cost of Merchandise Sold:					
Estimated Beginning Inventory, April 1					
Net Purchases					
Merchandise Available for Sale					
Less Estimated Ending Inventory, April 30					
Cost of Merchandise Sold					
Gross Profit on Operations					
Operating Expenses					
Net Income					

Preparing a stock record

STOCK RECORD						
Description 450-gallon spa				Stock No. HT-450		
Reorder 5		Minimum 2		Location Area A-4		
1	2	3	4	5	6	7
INCREASES			DECREASES			BALANCE
DATE	PURCHASE INVOICE NO.	QUANTITY	DATE	SALES INVOICE NO.	QUANTITY	QUANTITY
			Jan. 3	2399	1	4

19-2 APPLICATION PROBLEM, p. 578

Determining the cost of inventory using the fifo, lifo, and weighted-average inventory costing methods

FIFO Method

Purchase Dates	Units Purchased	Unit Price	Total Cost	FIFO Units on Hand	FIFO Cost
January 1, beginning inventory	90	$2.00	$180.00		
March 13, purchases	78	2.10	163.80		
June 8, purchases	80	2.25	180.00		
September 16, purchases	84	2.30	193.20		
December 22, purchases	88	2.40	211.20		
Totals	420		$928.20		

LIFO Method

Purchase Dates	Units Purchased	Unit Price	Total Cost	LIFO Units on Hand	LIFO Cost
January 1, beginning inventory	90	$2.00	$180.00		
March 13, purchases	78	2.10	163.80		
June 8, purchases	80	2.25	180.00		
September 16, purchases	84	2.30	193.20		
December 22, purchases	88	2.40	211.20		
Totals	420		$928.20		

Weighted-Average Method

Purchases			Total Cost
Date	Units	Unit Price	
January 1, beginning inventory	90	$2.00	
March 13, purchases	78	2.10	
June 8, purchases	80	2.25	
September 16, purchases	84	2.30	
December 22, purchases	88	2.40	
Totals	420		

Estimating ending inventory using the gross profit method

1.

STEP 1
Beginning inventory, March 1 . . . . _____
Plus net purchases for March 1 to March 31 . . . . _____
Equals cost of merchandise available for sale . . . . _____
STEP 2
Net sales for March 1 to March 31 . . . . _____
Times previous year's gross profit percentage . . . . _____
Equals estimated gross profit on operations . . . . _____
STEP 3
Net sales for March 1 to March 31 . . . . _____
Less estimated gross profit on operations . . . . _____
Equals estimated cost of merchandise sold . . . . _____
STEP 4
Cost of merchandise available for sale . . . . _____
Less estimated cost of merchandise sold . . . . _____
Equals estimated ending merchandise inventory . . . . _____

2.

Fultz Industries

Income Statement

For Month Ended March 31, 20 – –

					% OF NET SALES
Operating Revenue:					
Net Sales					
Cost of Merchandise Sold:					
Estimated Beginning Inventory, March 1					
Net Purchases					
Merchandise Available for Sale					
Less Estimated Ending Inventory, March 31					
Cost of Merchandise Sold					
Gross Profit on Operations					
Operating Expenses					
Net Income					

19-4 MASTERY PROBLEM, p. 579

Determining the cost of inventory using the fifo, lifo, and weighted-average inventory costing methods

1.

STOCK RECORD

Description Electronic switch _____   Stock No. P-234 _____

Reorder 20 _____   Minimum 10 _____   Location Aisle C-2 _____

1	2	3	4	5	6	7
INCREASES			DECREASES			BALANCE
DATE	PURCHASE INVOICE NO.	QUANTITY	DATE	SALES INVOICE NO.	QUANTITY	QUANTITY
			Jan. 1		8	8

2.

FIFO Method

Purchase Dates	Units Purchased	Unit Price	Total Cost	FIFO Units on Hand	FIFO Cost
January 1, beginning inventory	8	$4.98	$ 39.84		
January 6, purchases					
April 14, purchases					
August 3, purchases					
December 12, purchases					
Totals					

LIFO Method

Purchase Dates	Units Purchased	Unit Price	Total Cost	LIFO Units on Hand	LIFO Cost
January 1, beginning inventory	8	$4.98	$ 39.84		
January 6, purchases					
April 14, purchases					
August 3, purchases					
December 12, purchases					
Totals					

Weighted-Average Method

Purchases			Total Cost
Date	Units	Unit Price	
January 1, beginning inventory	8	$4.98	$ 39.84
January 6, purchases			
April 14, purchases			
August 3, purchases			
December 12, purchases			
Totals			

19-4 MASTERY PROBLEM (concluded)

3.

	Fifo	Lifo	Weighted-Average
Merchandise Available for Sale			
Ending Inventory			
Cost of Merchandise Sold			

Highest Cost of Merchandise Sold:

CHALLENGE PROBLEM, p. 580

Determining the cost of merchandise inventory destroyed in a fire

1.

Gross profit on operations . . . . _____

Divided by net sales . . . . _____

Equals gross profit percentage of net sales (prior year) . . . . _____

2.

STEP 1

  Beginning inventory, May 1 . . . . _____

  Plus net purchases for May 1 to May 12 . . . . _____

  Equals cost of merchandise available for sale . . . . _____

STEP 2

  Net sales for May 1 to May 12 . . . . _____

  Times previous year's gross profit percentage . . . . _____

  Equals estimated gross profit on operations . . . . _____

STEP 3

  Net sales for May 1 to May 12 . . . . _____

  Less estimated gross profit on operations . . . . _____

  Equals estimated cost of merchandise sold . . . . _____

STEP 4

  Cost of merchandise available for sale . . . . _____

  Less estimated cost of merchandise sold . . . . _____

  Equals estimated ending merchandise inventory . . . . _____

3.

Estimated merchandise inventory, May 12 . . . . _____

Less cost of merchandise inventory not destroyed . . . . _____

Equals estimated cost of merchandise inventory destroyed . . . . _____

4.

Murphy Electronics Company

Income Statement

For the Period May 1 to May 12, 20 – –

			% OF NET SALES
Operating Revenue:			
Net Sales			
Cost of Merchandise Sold:			
Estimated Beginning Inventory, May 1			
Net Purchases			
Merchandise Available for Sale			
Less Estimated Ending Inventory, May 12			
Cost of Merchandise Sold			
Gross Profit on Operations			
Operating Expenses			
Net Income			

19-5 **CHALLENGE PROBLEM (concluded)**

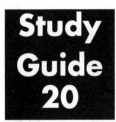

Study Guide 20

Name	Perfect Score	Your Score
Identifying Accounting Terms	18 Pts.	
Identifying Accounting Concepts and Practices	8 Pts.	
Analyzing Notes and Interest	8 Pts.	
Analyzing Notes Payable and Notes Receivable Transactions	14 Pts.	
Total	48 Pts.	

Part One—Identifying Accounting Terms

Directions: Select the one term in Column I that best fits each definition in Column II. Print the letter identifying your choice in the Answers column.

Column I	Column II	Answers
A. creditor	1. The number assigned to identify a specific note. (p. 589)	1. _____
B. current liabilities	2. The date a note is signed. (p. 589)	2. _____
C. date of a note	3. The person or business to whom the amount of a note is payable. (p. 589)	3. _____
D. dishonored note	4. The days, months, or years from the date of signing until a note is to be paid. (p. 589)	4. _____
E. interest	5. The original amount of a note. (p. 589)	5. _____
F. interest expense	6. The percentage of the principal that is paid for use of the money. (p. 589)	6. _____
G. interest income	7. The date a note is due. (p. 589)	7. _____
H. interest rate of a note	8. The person or business who signs a note and thus promises to make payment. (p. 589)	8. _____
I. maker of a note	9. A written and signed promise to pay a sum of money at a specified time. (p. 589)	9. _____
J. maturity date of a note	10. A person or organization to whom a liability is owed. (p. 589)	10. _____
K. maturity value	11. Promissory notes signed by a business and given to a creditor. (p. 589)	11. _____
L. notes payable	12. An amount paid for the use of money for a period of time. (p. 590)	12. _____
M. notes receivable	13. The amount that is due on the maturity date of a note. (p. 590)	13. _____
N. number of a note	14. Liabilities due within a short time, usually within a year. (p. 593)	14. _____
O. payee of a note	15. The interest accrued on money borrowed. (p. 594)	15. _____
P. principal of a note	16. Promissory notes that a business accepts from customers. (p. 598)	16. _____
Q. promissory note	17. The interest earned on money loaned. (p. 599)	17. _____
R. time of a note	18. A note that is not paid when due. (p. 600)	18. _____

Part Two—Identifying Accounting Concepts and Practices

Directions: Place a *T* for True or an *F* for False in the Answers column to show whether each of the following statements is true or false.

1. When the timing of cash receipts and required cash payments do not match, businesses usually deposit extra cash or borrow cash or make arrangements to delay payments. (p. 588)

   1. _____

2. "Interest at 12%" means that 12 cents will be paid for the use of each dollar borrowed for the time of a note. (p. 590)

   2. _____

3. An individual with a car loan usually pays the note in partial payments that include part of the principal and part of the interest on the note. (p. 590)

   3. _____

4. In interest calculations, time can be expressed in whole years or as a fraction of a year. (p. 590)

   4. _____

5. The maturity value of a note is calculated by subtracting the interest rate from the principal. (p. 590)

   5. _____

6. The journal entry for signing a note payable includes a debit to Interest Expense. (p. 593)

   6. _____

7. The journal entry for paying a note payable includes a debit to Accounts Payable to remove the balance owed. (p. 594)

   7. _____

8. When a note receivable is dishonored, the company should immediately write off the account receivable for that customer. (p. 600)

   8. _____

Part Three—Analyzing Notes and Interest

Directions: For each of the following items, select the choice that best completes the statement. Print the letter identifying your choice in the Answers column.

Answers

1. The most useful evidence of a debt in a court of law is (A) an oral promise to pay (B) an account receivable (C) an account payable (D) a signed note (p. 589)

   1. _____

2. The interest on a 180-day, 10% interest-bearing note of $2,000.00 is (A) $20.00 (B) $200.00 (C) $100.00 (D) none of these (p. 590)

   2. _____

3. The time of a note issued for less than one year is typically stated in (A) days (B) months (C) a fraction of a year (D) none of these (p. 590)

   3. _____

4. The maturity value of a 90-day, 12% interest-bearing note of $600.00 is (A) $582.00 (B) $672.00 (C) $624.00 (D) none of these (p. 590)

   4. _____

5. The maturity date of a 90-day note dated August 22 is (A) November 19 (B) November 20 (C) November 21 (D) November 22 (p. 591)

   5. _____

6. Notes payable are classified as (A) current assets (B) current liabilities (C) expenses (D) revenue (p. 593)

   6. _____

7. The source document for recording cash received from signing a note payable is a (A) receipt (B) check (C) memorandum (D) copy of the note (p. 593)

   7. _____

8. Notes receivable are classified as (A) other expense (B) current assets (C) current liabilities (D) other revenue (p. 598)

   8. _____

Part Four—Analyzing Notes Payable and Notes Receivable Transactions

Directions: Analyze each of the following transactions into debit and credit parts. Print the letter identifying your choices in the proper Answers column.

Account Titles	Transactions	Answers Debit	Credit
A. Accounts Payable	**1–2.** Signed a 90-day, 10% note. (p. 593)	**1.** _____	**2.** _____
B. Accounts Receivable			
C. Cash	**3–4.** Paid cash for the maturity value of a note plus interest. (p. 594)	**3.** _____	**4.** _____
D. Interest Expense			
E. Interest Income	**5–6.** Signed a 60-day, 18% note to Café on the Way for an extension of time on an account payable. (p. 595)	**5.** _____	**6.** _____
F. Notes Payable			
G. Notes Receivable	**7–8.** Paid cash for the maturity value of the note payable to Café on the Way. (p. 596)	**7.** _____	**8.** _____
	9–10. Accepted a 90-day, 18% note from Aimee Kane for an extension of time on her account. (p. 598)	**9.** _____	**10.** _____
ACCTS. RECEIVABLE LEDGER			
H. Aimee Kane	**11–12.** Received cash for the maturity value of the note receivable plus interest from Aimee Kane. (p. 599)	**11.** _____	**12.** _____
I. Common Grounds Coffee Shop			
ACCTS. PAYABLE LEDGER	**13–14.** Common Grounds Coffee Shop dishonored a note receivable, maturity value due today. (p. 600)	**13.** _____	**14.** _____
J. Café on the Way			

20-1 WORK TOGETHER, p. 592

Calculating interest, maturity dates, and maturity values for promissory notes

Date	Principal	Interest Rate	Time	Interest	Maturity Date	Maturity Value
March 3	$6,000.00	6%	90 days			
March 18	$2,000.00	9%	60 days			

Calculations:

Calculating interest, maturity dates, and maturity values for promissory notes

Date	Principal	Interest Rate	Time	Interest	Maturity Date	Maturity Value
June 8	$20,000.00	8%	180 days			
June 12	$10,000.00	6%	90 days			

Calculations:

20-2 **WORK TOGETHER, p. 597**

Journalizing notes payable transactions

1.

GENERAL JOURNAL

PAGE 3

DATE	ACCOUNT TITLE	DOC. NO.	POST. REF.	DEBIT	CREDIT

1.

CASH RECEIPTS JOURNAL

PAGE 5

				1 GENERAL	2	3 ACCOUNTS RECEIVABLE CREDIT	4 SALES CREDIT	5 SALES TAX PAYABLE CREDIT	6 SALES DISCOUNT DEBIT	7 CASH DEBIT
DATE	ACCOUNT TITLE	DOC. NO.	POST. REF.	DEBIT	CREDIT					

2.

CASH PAYMENTS JOURNAL

PAGE 9

				1 GENERAL	2	3 ACCOUNTS PAYABLE DEBIT	4 PURCHASES DISCOUNT CREDIT	5 CASH CREDIT
DATE	ACCOUNT TITLE	CK. NO.	POST. REF.	DEBIT	CREDIT			

Journalizing notes payable transactions

1.

GENERAL JOURNAL

PAGE 10

	DATE	ACCOUNT TITLE	DOC. NO.	POST. REF.	DEBIT	CREDIT	
1							1
2							2
3							3
4							4

1.

CASH RECEIPTS JOURNAL

PAGE 20

	DATE	ACCOUNT TITLE	DOC. NO.	POST. REF.	GENERAL DEBIT	GENERAL CREDIT	ACCOUNTS RECEIVABLE CREDIT	SALES CREDIT	SALES TAX PAYABLE CREDIT	SALES DISCOUNT DEBIT	CASH DEBIT	
					1	2	3	4	5	6	7	
1												1
2												2
3												3
4												4
5												5

2.

CASH PAYMENTS JOURNAL

PAGE 17

	DATE	ACCOUNT TITLE	CK. NO.	POST. REF.	GENERAL DEBIT	GENERAL CREDIT	ACCOUNTS PAYABLE DEBIT	PURCHASES DISCOUNT CREDIT	CASH CREDIT	
					1	2	3	4	5	
1										1
2										2
3										3
4										4
5										5

20-3 WORK TOGETHER, p. 602

Journalizing notes receivable transactions

GENERAL JOURNAL

PAGE 2

		DATE	ACCOUNT TITLE	DOC. NO.	POST. REF.	DEBIT	CREDIT	
1								1
2								2
3								3
4								4
5								5
6								6

CASH RECEIPTS JOURNAL

PAGE 3

	DATE	ACCOUNT TITLE	DOC. NO.	POST. REF.	GENERAL DEBIT	GENERAL CREDIT	ACCOUNTS RECEIVABLE CREDIT	SALES CREDIT	SALES TAX PAYABLE CREDIT	SALES DISCOUNT DEBIT	CASH DEBIT	
1												1
2												2
3												3
4												4
5												5

Journalizing notes receivable transactions

GENERAL JOURNAL

PAGE 3

DATE	ACCOUNT TITLE	DOC. NO.	POST. REF.	DEBIT	CREDIT
						1
						2
						3
						4
						5
						6

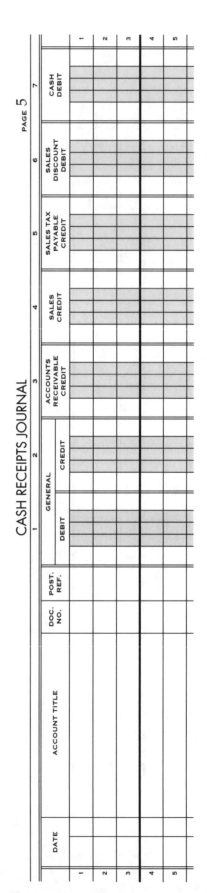

CASH RECEIPTS JOURNAL

PAGE 5

20-1 APPLICATION PROBLEM, p. 604

Calculating interest, maturity dates, and maturity values for promissory notes

Date	Principal	Interest Rate	Time	Interest	Maturity Date	Maturity Value
April 6	$10,000.00	12%	180 days			
April 12	$600.00	9%	60 days			
April 15	$5,000.00	10%	90 days			
April 23	$3,000.00	14%	60 days			

Calculations:

Journalizing notes payable transactions

1.

GENERAL JOURNAL

PAGE 4

DATE	ACCOUNT TITLE	DOC. NO.	POST. REF.	DEBIT	CREDIT	
						1
						2
						3
						4
						5
						6

CASH RECEIPTS JOURNAL

PAGE 6

| | | | | 1 | 2 | 3 | 4 | 5 | 6 | 7 |
| | | | | GENERAL | | ACCOUNTS RECEIVABLE CREDIT | SALES CREDIT | SALES TAX PAYABLE CREDIT | SALES DISCOUNT DEBIT | CASH DEBIT |
DATE	ACCOUNT TITLE	DOC. NO.	POST. REF.	DEBIT	CREDIT					

20-2 **APPLICATION PROBLEM (concluded)**

2.

CASH PAYMENTS JOURNAL

PAGE 9

DATE	ACCOUNT TITLE	CK. NO.	POST. REF.	GENERAL DEBIT	GENERAL CREDIT	ACCOUNTS PAYABLE DEBIT	PURCHASES DISCOUNT CREDIT	CASH CREDIT
				1	2	3	4	5
								1
								2
								3
								4
								5
								6
								7
								8
								9
								10
								11
								12
								13
								14
								15
								16
								17
								18
								19
								20
								21
								22
								23
								24

Journalizing notes receivable transactions

GENERAL JOURNAL   PAGE 14

	DATE	ACCOUNT TITLE	DOC. NO.	POST. REF.	DEBIT	CREDIT	
1							1
2							2
3							3
4							4
5							5
6							6
7							7
8							8
9							9
10							10
11							11
12							12
13							13
14							14
15							15
16							16
17							17
18							18
19							19
20							20
21							21
22							22
23							23
24							24
25							25
26							26
27							27
28							28
29							29
30							30
31							31
32							32
33							33

20-3 **APPLICATION PROBLEM (concluded)**

CASH RECEIPTS JOURNAL

PAGE 10

	DATE	ACCOUNT TITLE	DOC. NO.	POST. REF.	GENERAL DEBIT	GENERAL CREDIT	ACCOUNTS RECEIVABLE CREDIT	SALES CREDIT	SALES TAX PAYABLE CREDIT	SALES DISCOUNT DEBIT	CASH DEBIT	
					1	2	3	4	5	6	7	
1												1
2												2
3												3
4												4
5												5
6												6
7												7
8												8
9												9
10												10
11												11
12												12
13												13
14												14
15												15
16												16
17												17
18												18
19												19
20												20
21												21
22												22
23												23
24												24
25												25

Journalizing notes receivable transactions

GENERAL JOURNAL   PAGE 18

	DATE		ACCOUNT TITLE	DOC. NO.	POST. REF.	DEBIT	CREDIT	
1								1
2								2
3								3
4								4
5								5
6								6
7								7
8								8
9								9
10								10
11								11
12								12
13								13
14								14
15								15
16								16
17								17
18								18
19								19
20								20
21								21
22								22
23								23
24								24
25								25
26								26
27								27
28								28
29								29
30								30
31								31
32								32
33								33

20-4 **APPLICATION PROBLEM (concluded)**

CASH RECEIPTS JOURNAL

PAGE 11

			GENERAL		ACCOUNTS RECEIVABLE CREDIT	SALES CREDIT	SALES TAX PAYABLE CREDIT	SALES DISCOUNT DEBIT	CASH DEBIT
DATE	ACCOUNT TITLE	DOC. NO.	POST. REF.	DEBIT	CREDIT					
				1	2	3	4	5	6	7

Journalizing notes payable and notes receivable transactions

1.

GENERAL JOURNAL

PAGE 7

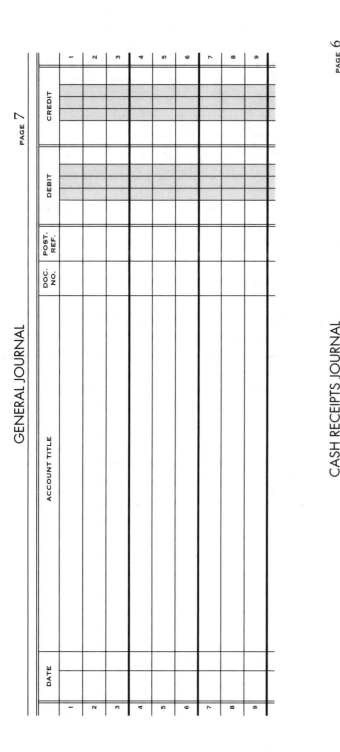

DATE	ACCOUNT TITLE	DOC. NO.	POST. REF.	DEBIT	CREDIT	
						1
						2
						3
						4
						5
						6
						7
						8
						9

CASH RECEIPTS JOURNAL

PAGE 6

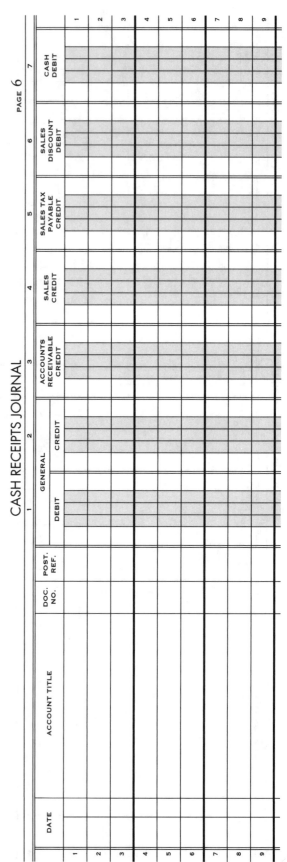

				1	2	3	4	5	6	7	
DATE	ACCOUNT TITLE	DOC. NO.	POST. REF.	GENERAL DEBIT	GENERAL CREDIT	ACCOUNTS RECEIVABLE CREDIT	SALES CREDIT	SALES TAX PAYABLE CREDIT	SALES DISCOUNT DEBIT	CASH DEBIT	
											1
											2
											3
											4
											5
											6
											7
											8
											9

20-5 MASTERY PROBLEM (continued)

2.

3.

CASH PAYMENTS JOURNAL

PAGE 9

	DATE	ACCOUNT TITLE	CK. NO.	POST. REF.	GENERAL DEBIT 1	GENERAL CREDIT 2	ACCOUNTS PAYABLE DEBIT 3	PURCHASES DISCOUNT CREDIT 4	CASH CREDIT 5
1									
2									
3									
4									
5									
6									
7									
8									
9									
10									
11									
12									
13									
14									
15									
16									
17									
18									
19									
20									
21									
22									
23									
24									

20-6 CHALLENGE PROBLEM, p. 606

Recording notes receivable stated in months

1.

2.

3.

4.

REINFORCEMENT ACTIVITY 3 PART A, pp. 610–613

An accounting cycle for a corporation: journalizing and posting transactions

1.

GENERAL JOURNAL

	DATE		ACCOUNT TITLE	DOC. NO.	POST. REF.	DEBIT	CREDIT	
1								1
2								2
3								3
4								4
5								5
6								6
7								7
8								8
9								9
10								10
11								11
12								12
13								13
14								14
15								15
16								16
17								17
18								18
19								19
20								20
21								21
22								22
23								23
24								24
25								25
26								26
27								27
28								28
29								29
30								30
31								31
32								32

REINFORCEMENT ACTIVITY 3 PART A (continued)

1., 2.

SALES JOURNAL

PAGE 12

	DATE		ACCOUNT DEBITED	SALE NO.	POST. REF.	ACCOUNTS RECEIVABLE DEBIT	SALES CREDIT	SALES TAX PAYABLE CREDIT	
						1	2	3	
1									1
2									2
3									3
4									4
5									5
6									6
7									7
8									8
9									9
10									10
11									11
12									12
13									13
14									14
15									15
16									16
17									17
18									18

REINFORCEMENT ACTIVITY 3 PART A (continued)

1., 3.

PURCHASES JOURNAL   PAGE 12

	DATE		ACCOUNT CREDITED	PURCH. NO.	POST. REF.	PURCHASES DR. ACCTS. PAY. CR.	
1							1
2							2
3							3
4							4
5							5
6							6
7							7
8							8
9							9
10							10
11							11
12							12
13							13
14							14
15							15
16							16
17							17
18							18
19							19
20							20
21							21
22							22
23							23
24							24
25							25

1., 4., 6.

CASH RECEIPTS JOURNAL

PAGE 12

	DATE	ACCOUNT TITLE	DOC. NO.	POST. REF.	1 GENERAL DEBIT	2 GENERAL CREDIT	3 ACCOUNTS RECEIVABLE CREDIT	4 SALES CREDIT	5 SALES TAX PAYABLE CREDIT	6 SALES DISCOUNT DEBIT	7 CASH DEBIT	
1												1
2												2
3												3
4												4
5												5
6												6
7												7
8												8
9												9
10												10
11												11
12												12
13												13
14												14
15												15
16												16
17												17
18												18
19												19

5.

CASH PROOF

Cash on hand at the beginning of the month . . . . _____

Plus total cash received during the month . . . . _____

Equals total . . . . _____

Less total cash paid during the month . . . . _____

Equals cash balance on hand at end of the month . . . . _____

Checkbook balance on the next unused check stub . . . . _____

REINFORCEMENT ACTIVITY 3 PART A (continued)

1., 4., 7.

CASH PAYMENTS JOURNAL   PAGE 23

	DATE		ACCOUNT TITLE	CK. NO.	POST. REF.	GENERAL DEBIT	GENERAL CREDIT	ACCOUNTS PAYABLE DEBIT	PURCHASES DISCOUNT CREDIT	CASH CREDIT	
1											1
2											2
3											3
4											4
5											5
6											6
7											7
8											8
9											9
10											10
11											11
12											12
13											13
14											14
15											15
16											16
17											17
18											18
19											19
20											20
21											21
22											22
23											23
24											24
25											25
26											26
27											27
28											28
29											29
30											30
31											31
32											32

1., 9.

PLANT ASSET RECORD No. __432__		General Ledger Account No. __1215__

Description __Hand Truck__   General Ledger Account __Warehouse Equip.__

Date
Bought __January 5, 20X1__   Serial Number __215-225__   Original Cost __$2,900.00__

Estimated
Useful Life __5 years__   Estimated Salvage Value __$500.00__   Depreciation Method __Straight-line__

Disposed of: Discarded _____   Sold _____   Traded _____
Date _____   Disposal Amount _____

Year	Annual Depreciation Expense	Accumulated Depreciation	Ending Book Value
20X1	$480.00	$ 480.00	$2,420.00
20X2	480.00	960.00	1,940.00
20X3	480.00	1,440.00	1,460.00

PLANT ASSET RECORD No. __667__		General Ledger Account No. __1205__

Description __Computer Printer__   General Ledger Account __Office Equipment__

Date
Bought __April 5, 20X1__   Serial Number __BE35CC__   Original Cost __$850.00__

Estimated
Useful Life __3 years__   Estimated Salvage Value __$130.00__   Depreciation Method __Straight-line__

Disposed of: Discarded _____   Sold _____   Traded _____
Date _____   Disposal Amount _____

Year	Annual Depreciation Expense	Accumulated Depreciation	Ending Book Value
20X2	$180.00	$180.00	$670.00
20X3	240.00	420.00	430.00

REINFORCEMENT ACTIVITY 3 PART A (continued)

PLANT ASSET RECORD No. _____   General Ledger Account No. _____

Description _____   General Ledger Account _____

Date   Serial
Bought _____ Number _____ Original Cost _____

                        Estimated
Estimated   Salvage   Depreciation
Useful Life _____ Value _____   Method _____

Disposed of: Discarded _____ Sold _____ Traded _____
Date _____   Disposal Amount _____

Year	Annual Depreciation Expense	Accumulated Depreciation	Ending Book Value

REINFORCEMENT ACTIVITY 3 PART A (continued)

1.

ACCOUNTS RECEIVABLE LEDGER

CUSTOMER Baker & Associates   **CUSTOMER NO.** 110

DATE	ITEM	POST. REF.	DEBIT	CREDIT	DEBIT BALANCE

CUSTOMER Felton Industries   **CUSTOMER NO.** 120

DATE	ITEM	POST. REF.	DEBIT	CREDIT	DEBIT BALANCE
20-- Dec. 1	Balance	✔			2 4 6 0 00

CUSTOMER Hilldale School   **CUSTOMER NO.** 130

DATE	ITEM	POST. REF.	DEBIT	CREDIT	DEBIT BALANCE
20-- Dec. 1	Balance	✔			2 4 3 00

CUSTOMER Horton Company   **CUSTOMER NO.** 140

DATE	ITEM	POST. REF.	DEBIT	CREDIT	DEBIT BALANCE

CUSTOMER Nelson Co.   **CUSTOMER NO.** 150

DATE	ITEM	POST. REF.	DEBIT	CREDIT	DEBIT BALANCE
20-- Dec. 1	Balance	✔			3 6 0 0 00

REINFORCEMENT ACTIVITY 3 PART A (continued)

CUSTOMER Ruocco Plastics   CUSTOMER NO. 160

DATE		ITEM	POST. REF.	DEBIT	CREDIT	DEBIT BALANCE
20-- Dec.	1	Balance	✔			3 2 5 0 00

8.

				DEBIT BALANCE

REINFORCEMENT ACTIVITY 3 PART A (continued)

1.

ACCOUNTS PAYABLE LEDGER

VENDOR Buntin Supply Company — VENDOR NO. 210

DATE		ITEM	POST. REF.	DEBIT	CREDIT	CREDIT BALANCE
20-- Dec.	1	Balance	✔			1 2 7 2 00

VENDOR Draper Company — VENDOR NO. 220

DATE		ITEM	POST. REF.	DEBIT	CREDIT	CREDIT BALANCE
20-- Dec.	1	Balance	✔			1 4 1 7 25

VENDOR Glenson Company — VENDOR NO. 230

DATE		ITEM	POST. REF.	DEBIT	CREDIT	CREDIT BALANCE
20-- Dec.	1	Balance	✔			1 9 8 00

VENDOR Hinsdale Supply Co. — VENDOR NO. 240

DATE	ITEM	POST. REF.	DEBIT	CREDIT	CREDIT BALANCE

VENDOR SHF Corp. — VENDOR NO. 250

DATE		ITEM	POST. REF.	DEBIT	CREDIT	CREDIT BALANCE
20-- Dec.	1	Balance	✔			5 8 0 00

REINFORCEMENT ACTIVITY 3 PART A (continued)

VENDOR Walbash Manufacturing   VENDOR NO. 260

DATE		ITEM	POST. REF.	DEBIT	CREDIT	CREDIT BALANCE
20-- Dec.	1	Balance	✔			6 2 0 00

8.

REINFORCEMENT ACTIVITY 3 PART A (continued)

1., 2., 3., 6., 7., 18., 19., 21.

GENERAL LEDGER

ACCOUNT Cash   ACCOUNT NO. 1105

DATE		ITEM	POST. REF.	DEBIT	CREDIT	BALANCE DEBIT	BALANCE CREDIT
20-- Dec.	1	Balance	✔			3 9 5 9 80	

ACCOUNT Petty Cash   ACCOUNT NO. 1110

DATE		ITEM	POST. REF.	DEBIT	CREDIT	BALANCE DEBIT	BALANCE CREDIT
20-- Dec.	1	Balance	✔			2 0 0 00	

ACCOUNT Notes Receivable   ACCOUNT NO. 1115

DATE		ITEM	POST. REF.	DEBIT	CREDIT	BALANCE DEBIT	BALANCE CREDIT
20-- Dec.	1	Balance	✔			8 8 0 0 00	

ACCOUNT Interest Receivable   ACCOUNT NO. 1120

DATE		ITEM	POST. REF.	DEBIT	CREDIT	BALANCE DEBIT	BALANCE CREDIT

ACCOUNT Accounts Receivable   ACCOUNT NO. 1125

DATE		ITEM	POST. REF.	DEBIT	CREDIT	BALANCE DEBIT	BALANCE CREDIT
20-- Dec.	1	Balance	✔			9 5 5 3 00	

REINFORCEMENT ACTIVITY 3 PART A (continued)

ACCOUNT Allowance for Uncollectible Accounts   ACCOUNT NO. 1130

DATE		ITEM	POST. REF.	DEBIT	CREDIT	BALANCE	
						DEBIT	CREDIT
20-- Dec.	1	Balance	✔				4 2 60

ACCOUNT Merchandise Inventory   ACCOUNT NO. 1135

DATE		ITEM	POST. REF.	DEBIT	CREDIT	BALANCE	
						DEBIT	CREDIT
20-- Dec.	1	Balance	✔			74 1 7 6 95	

ACCOUNT Supplies   ACCOUNT NO. 1140

DATE		ITEM	POST. REF.	DEBIT	CREDIT	BALANCE	
						DEBIT	CREDIT
20-- Dec.	1	Balance	✔			2 5 0 1 15	

ACCOUNT Prepaid Insurance   ACCOUNT NO. 1145

DATE		ITEM	POST. REF.	DEBIT	CREDIT	BALANCE	
						DEBIT	CREDIT
20-- Dec.	1	Balance	✔			8 6 0 0 00	

ACCOUNT Office Equipment   ACCOUNT NO. 1205

DATE		ITEM	POST. REF.	DEBIT	CREDIT	BALANCE	
						DEBIT	CREDIT
20-- Dec.	1	Balance	✔			23 4 8 0 00	

ACCOUNT Accumulated Depreciation—Office Equipment   ACCOUNT NO. 1210

DATE		ITEM	POST. REF.	DEBIT	CREDIT	BALANCE DEBIT	BALANCE CREDIT
20-- Dec.	1	Balance	✔				7 5 8 0 00

ACCOUNT Warehouse Equipment   ACCOUNT NO. 1215

DATE		ITEM	POST. REF.	DEBIT	CREDIT	BALANCE DEBIT	BALANCE CREDIT
20-- Dec.	1	Balance	✔			29 0 1 0 00	

ACCOUNT Accumulated Depreciation—Warehouse Equipment   ACCOUNT NO. 1220

DATE		ITEM	POST. REF.	DEBIT	CREDIT	BALANCE DEBIT	BALANCE CREDIT
20-- Dec.	1	Balance	✔				8 4 8 0 00

ACCOUNT Notes Payable   ACCOUNT NO. 2105

DATE		ITEM	POST. REF.	DEBIT	CREDIT	BALANCE DEBIT	BALANCE CREDIT
20-- Dec.	1	Balance	✔				20 0 0 0 00

ACCOUNT Interest Payable   ACCOUNT NO. 2110

DATE		ITEM	POST. REF.	DEBIT	CREDIT	BALANCE DEBIT	BALANCE CREDIT

REINFORCEMENT ACTIVITY 3 PART A (continued)

ACCOUNT Accounts Payable   ACCOUNT NO. 2115

DATE		ITEM	POST. REF.	DEBIT	CREDIT	BALANCE	
						DEBIT	CREDIT
Dec. 20--	1	Balance	✔				4 0 8 7 25

ACCOUNT Federal Income Tax Payable   ACCOUNT NO. 2120

DATE		ITEM	POST. REF.	DEBIT	CREDIT	BALANCE	
						DEBIT	CREDIT

ACCOUNT Employee Income Tax Payable   ACCOUNT NO. 2125

DATE		ITEM	POST. REF.	DEBIT	CREDIT	BALANCE	
						DEBIT	CREDIT
Dec. 20--	1	Balance	✔				3 2 4 00

ACCOUNT Social Security Tax Payable   ACCOUNT NO. 2130

DATE		ITEM	POST. REF.	DEBIT	CREDIT	BALANCE	
						DEBIT	CREDIT
Dec. 20--	1	Balance	✔				7 4 2 00

REINFORCEMENT ACTIVITY 3 PART A (continued)

ACCOUNT Medicare Tax Payable   ACCOUNT NO. 2135

DATE		ITEM	POST. REF.	DEBIT	CREDIT	BALANCE	
						DEBIT	CREDIT
Dec.	1	Balance	✔				1 6 2 35

ACCOUNT Sales Tax Payable   ACCOUNT NO. 2140

DATE		ITEM	POST. REF.	DEBIT	CREDIT	BALANCE	
						DEBIT	CREDIT
Dec.	1	Balance	✔				4 9 4 2 68

ACCOUNT Unemployment Tax Payable—Federal   ACCOUNT NO. 2145

DATE		ITEM	POST. REF.	DEBIT	CREDIT	BALANCE	
						DEBIT	CREDIT
Dec.	1	Balance	✔				1 3 05

ACCOUNT Unemployment Tax Payable—State   ACCOUNT NO. 2150

DATE		ITEM	POST. REF.	DEBIT	CREDIT	BALANCE	
						DEBIT	CREDIT
Dec.	1	Balance	✔				8 8 05

ACCOUNT Health Insurance Premiums Payable   ACCOUNT NO. 2155

DATE		ITEM	POST. REF.	DEBIT	CREDIT	BALANCE	
						DEBIT	CREDIT
Dec.	1	Balance	✔				7 2 5 00

REINFORCEMENT ACTIVITY 3 PART A (continued)

ACCOUNT Dividends Payable   ACCOUNT NO. 2160

DATE		ITEM	POST. REF.	DEBIT	CREDIT	BALANCE	
						DEBIT	CREDIT
Dec. 20--	1	Balance	✔				5 0 0 0 00

ACCOUNT Capital Stock   ACCOUNT NO. 3105

DATE		ITEM	POST. REF.	DEBIT	CREDIT	BALANCE	
						DEBIT	CREDIT
Dec. 20--	1	Balance	✔				30 0 0 0 00

ACCOUNT Retained Earnings   ACCOUNT NO. 3110

DATE		ITEM	POST. REF.	DEBIT	CREDIT	BALANCE	
						DEBIT	CREDIT
Dec. 20--	1	Balance	✔				23 8 8 9 20

ACCOUNT Dividends   ACCOUNT NO. 3115

DATE		ITEM	POST. REF.	DEBIT	CREDIT	BALANCE	
						DEBIT	CREDIT
Dec. 20--	1	Balance	✔			20 0 0 0 00	

ACCOUNT Income Summary   ACCOUNT NO. 3120

DATE		ITEM	POST. REF.	DEBIT	CREDIT	BALANCE	
						DEBIT	CREDIT

ACCOUNT Sales   ACCOUNT NO. 4105

DATE		ITEM	POST. REF.	DEBIT	CREDIT	BALANCE	
						DEBIT	CREDIT
Dec. 20--	1	Balance	✔				756 3 9 7 90

REINFORCEMENT ACTIVITY 3 PART A (continued)

ACCOUNT Sales Discount   ACCOUNT NO. 4110

DATE		ITEM	POST. REF.	DEBIT	CREDIT	BALANCE DEBIT	BALANCE CREDIT
20-- Dec.	1	Balance	✔			1 8 7 8 60	

ACCOUNT Sales Returns and Allowances   ACCOUNT NO. 4115

DATE		ITEM	POST. REF.	DEBIT	CREDIT	BALANCE DEBIT	BALANCE CREDIT
20-- Dec.	1	Balance	✔			6 0 5 4 80	

ACCOUNT Purchases   ACCOUNT NO. 5105

DATE		ITEM	POST. REF.	DEBIT	CREDIT	BALANCE DEBIT	BALANCE CREDIT
20-- Dec.	1	Balance	✔			506 3 5 4 40	

ACCOUNT Purchases Discount   ACCOUNT NO. 5110

DATE		ITEM	POST. REF.	DEBIT	CREDIT	BALANCE DEBIT	BALANCE CREDIT
20-- Dec.	1	Balance	✔				3 4 9 3 32

ACCOUNT Purchases Returns and Allowances   ACCOUNT NO. 5115

DATE		ITEM	POST. REF.	DEBIT	CREDIT	BALANCE DEBIT	BALANCE CREDIT
20-- Dec.	1	Balance	✔				3 0 3 8 00

REINFORCEMENT ACTIVITY 3 PART A (continued)

ACCOUNT Advertising Expense   ACCOUNT NO. 6105

DATE	ITEM	POST. REF.	DEBIT	CREDIT	BALANCE DEBIT	BALANCE CREDIT
Dec. 1	Balance	✔			9 5 5 6 70	

ACCOUNT Cash Short and Over   ACCOUNT NO. 6110

DATE	ITEM	POST. REF.	DEBIT	CREDIT	BALANCE DEBIT	BALANCE CREDIT
Dec. 1	Balance	✔			2 0 00	

ACCOUNT Credit Card Fee Expense   ACCOUNT NO. 6115

DATE	ITEM	POST. REF.	DEBIT	CREDIT	BALANCE DEBIT	BALANCE CREDIT
Dec. 1	Balance	✔			14 1 1 1 40	

ACCOUNT Depreciation Expense—Office Equipment   ACCOUNT NO. 6120

DATE	ITEM	POST. REF.	DEBIT	CREDIT	BALANCE DEBIT	BALANCE CREDIT

ACCOUNT Depreciation Expense—Warehouse Equipment   ACCOUNT NO. 6125

DATE	ITEM	POST. REF.	DEBIT	CREDIT	BALANCE DEBIT	BALANCE CREDIT

REINFORCEMENT ACTIVITY 3 PART A (continued)

ACCOUNT Insurance Expense   ACCOUNT NO. 6130

DATE	ITEM	POST. REF.	DEBIT	CREDIT	BALANCE	
					DEBIT	CREDIT

ACCOUNT Miscellaneous Expense   ACCOUNT NO. 6135

DATE	ITEM	POST. REF.	DEBIT	CREDIT	BALANCE	
					DEBIT	CREDIT
20-- Dec. 1	Balance	✔			5 7 3 3 95	

ACCOUNT Payroll Taxes Expense   ACCOUNT NO. 6140

DATE	ITEM	POST. REF.	DEBIT	CREDIT	BALANCE	
					DEBIT	CREDIT
20-- Dec. 1	Balance	✔			10 1 7 6 85	

ACCOUNT Rent Expense   ACCOUNT NO. 6145

DATE	ITEM	POST. REF.	DEBIT	CREDIT	BALANCE	
					DEBIT	CREDIT
20-- Dec. 1	Balance	✔			19 2 5 0 00	

ACCOUNT Repairs Expense   ACCOUNT NO. 6150

DATE	ITEM	POST. REF.	DEBIT	CREDIT	BALANCE	
					DEBIT	CREDIT
20-- Dec.	Balance	✔			1 3 9 4 80	

REINFORCEMENT ACTIVITY 3 PART A (continued)

ACCOUNT Salary Expense   ACCOUNT NO. 6155

DATE	ITEM	POST. REF.	DEBIT	CREDIT	BALANCE DEBIT	BALANCE CREDIT
20-- Dec. 1	Balance	✔			99 29 8 00	

ACCOUNT Supplies Expense   ACCOUNT NO. 6160

DATE	ITEM	POST. REF.	DEBIT	CREDIT	BALANCE DEBIT	BALANCE CREDIT

ACCOUNT Uncollectible Accounts Expense   ACCOUNT NO. 6165

DATE	ITEM	POST. REF.	DEBIT	CREDIT	BALANCE DEBIT	BALANCE CREDIT

ACCOUNT Utilities Expense   ACCOUNT NO. 6170

DATE	ITEM	POST. REF.	DEBIT	CREDIT	BALANCE DEBIT	BALANCE CREDIT
20-- Dec. 1	Balance	✔			6 89 0 00	

ACCOUNT Gain on Plant Assets   ACCOUNT NO. 7105

DATE	ITEM	POST. REF.	DEBIT	CREDIT	BALANCE DEBIT	BALANCE CREDIT
20-- Dec. 1	Balance	✔				3 65 00

ACCOUNT Interest Income   ACCOUNT NO. 7110

DATE		ITEM	POST. REF.	DEBIT	CREDIT	BALANCE DEBIT	BALANCE CREDIT
20-- Dec.	1	Balance	✔				1 8 0 00

ACCOUNT Interest Expense   ACCOUNT NO. 8105

DATE		ITEM	POST. REF.	DEBIT	CREDIT	BALANCE DEBIT	BALANCE CREDIT
20-- Dec.	1	Balance	✔			2 3 0 0 00	

ACCOUNT Loss on Plant Assets   ACCOUNT NO. 8110

DATE		ITEM	POST. REF.	DEBIT	CREDIT	BALANCE DEBIT	BALANCE CREDIT
20-- Dec.	1	Balance	✔			2 5 0 00	

ACCOUNT Federal Income Tax Expense   ACCOUNT NO. 9105

DATE		ITEM	POST. REF.	DEBIT	CREDIT	BALANCE DEBIT	BALANCE CREDIT
20-- Dec.	1	Balance	✔			6 0 0 0 00	

Study Guide 21

Name	Perfect Score	Your Score
Identifying Accounting Concepts and Practices	15 Pts.	
Analyzing Accounts Affected by Accrued Revenue and Accrued Expenses	18 Pts.	
Analyzing Accrued Revenue and Accrued Expenses	11 Pts.	
Total	44 Pts.	

Part One—Identifying Accounting Concepts and Practices

Directions: For each of the following items, select the choice that best completes the statement. Print the letter identifying your choice in the Answers column.

Answers

1. At the end of a fiscal period, each expense that has been incurred but not paid should be recorded as (A) an adjusting entry (B) a reversing entry (C) a closing entry (D) an opening entry. (p. 616)

    1. _____

2. Revenue earned in one fiscal period but not received until a later fiscal period is called (A) accrued expense (B) accrued interest expense (C) accrued revenue (D) deferred interest income. (p. 616)

    2. _____

3. Recording adjusting entries for the fiscal period in which the revenue has been earned regardless of when it will be received is an application of the accounting concept (A) Objective Evidence (B) Realization of Revenue (C) Adequate Disclosure (D) Historical Cost. (p. 616)

    3. _____

4. At the end of a fiscal period, any revenue that has been earned but not received should be credited to an appropriate (A) revenue account (B) expense account (C) liability account (D) asset account. (p. 616)

    4. _____

5. Interest earned but not yet received is called (A) accrued interest income (B) deferred interest income (C) deferred earned income (D) none of these. (p. 617)

    5. _____

6. Interest Receivable is (A) an asset (B) a liability (C) revenue (D) an expense. (p. 618)

    6. _____

7. An entry made at the beginning of one fiscal period to reverse an adjusting entry made in the previous fiscal period is called (A) a debit entry (B) a credit entry (C) a reversing entry (D) none of these. (p. 619)

    7. _____

8. A reversing entry for accrued interest income results in a debit to (A) Interest Receivable (B) Notes Receivable (C) Income Summary (D) Interest Income. (p. 619)

    8. _____

9. A reversing entry for accrued interest income will result in an account balance of (A) Interest Receivable debit (B) Interest Income debit (C) Interest Receivable credit (D) Interest Income credit. (p. 619)

    9. _____

10. Expenses incurred in one fiscal period but not paid until a later fiscal period are called (A) accrued interest expenses (B) accrued expenses (C) accrued income expenses (D) accrued interest receivable. (p. 622)

    10. _____

11. At the end of a fiscal period, each expense that has been incurred but not paid should be debited to an appropriate (A) revenue account (B) expense account (C) asset account (D) liability account. (p. 622)

    11. _____

12. Interest incurred but not yet paid is called (A) accrued income expense (B) earned income (C) accrued interest expense (D) deferred interest expense. (p. 622)

    12. _____

13. At the end of a fiscal period, each expense that has been incurred but not paid should be credited to an appropriate (A) revenue account (B) expense account (C) asset account (D) liability account. (p. 622)

    13. _____

14. A reversing entry for accrued interest expense will result in an account balance of (A) Interest Payable debit (B) Interest Payable credit (C) Interest Expense debit (D) Interest Expense credit. (p. 624)

    14. _____

15. An adjusting entry normally is reversed if the adjusting entry creates a balance in (A) a revenue or expense account (B) a revenue and liability account (C) an expense and asset account (D) an asset or liability account. (p. 626)

    15. _____

Part Two—Analyzing Accounts Affected by Accrued Revenue and Accrued Expenses

Directions: Analyze each of the following entries into debit and credit parts. Print the letter identifying your choice in the proper Answers columns. Determine in which journal each of the transactions are to be recorded.

G—General journal   CP—Cash payments journal   CR—Cash receipts journal

Account Titles	Transactions	Journal	Answers Debit	Credit
A. Cash	1–2–3. Recorded an adjustment for accrued interest income. (p. 617)	1. _____	2. _____	3. _____
B. Interest Expense	4–5–6. Reversed an adjusting entry for accrued interest income. (p. 619)	4. _____	5. _____	6. _____
C. Interest Income	7–8–9. Received cash for the maturity value of a 90-day, 12% note. (p. 620)	7. _____	8. _____	9. _____
D. Interest Payable	10–11–12. Recorded an adjustment for accrued interest expense. (p. 622)	10. _____	11. _____	12. _____
E. Interest Receivable	13–14–15. Reversed an adjusting entry for accrued interest expense. (p. 624)	13. _____	14. _____	15. _____
F. Notes Payable	16–17–18. Paid cash for the maturity value of a note payable plus interest. (p. 625)	16. _____	17. _____	18. _____
G. Notes Receivable				

Part Three—Analyzing Accrued Revenue and Accrued Expenses

Directions: Place a *T* for True or an *F* for False in the Answers column to show whether each of the following statements is true or false.

	Answers
1. Revenue should be recorded when the revenue is earned. (p. 616)	1. _____
2. Adjusting entries are made at the beginning of each fiscal period. (p. 616)	2. _____
3. The adjustment for accrued interest income is planned on a work sheet. (p. 617)	3. _____
4. Accrued interest income is credited to the interest income account. (p. 617)	4. _____
5. When an adjusting entry for accrued interest income is made, Interest Receivable is debited. (p. 617)	5. _____
6. Accrued interest is calculated by multiplying principal times interest rate times time as a fraction of a year. (p. 617)	6. _____
7. Reversing entries are made on the last day of the fiscal period. (p. 619)	7. _____
8. A reversing entry for interest income reduces the balance of Interest Receivable. (p. 619)	8. _____
9. At the end of a fiscal period, the Interest Expense balance after adjustments shows the amount of interest expense that has been incurred in that fiscal period. (p. 622)	9. _____
10. An Interest Payable credit balance is accrued interest expense incurred in the current year but to be paid in the next year. (p. 622)	10. _____
11. When a reversing entry is made for accrued interest expense, a debit entry is required to Interest Payable. (p. 624)	11. _____

Study Skills

Following Directions

"I thought you said the paper was due next week."
"Isn't this what I was supposed to do?"
"When did you tell us to do that?"

These are remarks often heard at school. A student has missed a deadline; another has done the wrong assignment; a third did not recall receiving the assignment at all. All three will receive a poor grade when they could easily have made a good grade. Why? The reason is that they did not listen to directions or they did not follow directions.

Listen Attentively

In order to meet all deadlines, you must listen very carefully when an assignment is made. Your teacher will probably give complete directions, including due date. If any part of the assignment is not clear, you should ask for a clarification when the assignment is made. If you have any doubt about the format, the content, or the due date, you should ask immediately. Do not wait to ask until it is time to turn in the assignment. You may miss the deadline altogether, or you may not allow yourself enough time to complete the assignment properly.

Follow Directions to the Letter

You must complete each assignment according to the directions your teacher gives. For example, you may be asked to write a major paper. Your teacher will probably give you detailed instructions on how information is to be collected and how it is to be presented in the paper.

If your teacher asks you to obtain references from at least three books, be sure that you do. Four books will be satisfactory, but two will not. If asked to use current references, articles three or four years old will not be satisfactory. If your teacher asks you to use charts and graphs to illustrate your points, be sure that you include them.

Use the Right Format

There are many formats that are acceptable for preparing most assignments. If your teacher asks you to use a specific format, you must follow it, even if you prefer another. If no format is specified for a writing assignment, you should ask. If there is no preference, you should use a simple format and be completely consistent.

Right on Schedule

If you have a major assignment given to you at the beginning of the term, begin work early, following all directions. If you leave all the work to do at the last minute, the quality will suffer and so will your grade. It is not usually possible to collect a large amount of information overnight. In addition, if you try to do all your work just before it is due, you will have no time to reflect on the work and change any part that you do not like.

Be absolutely sure to turn your assignment in right on schedule. It should not be necessary for you to ask for extra time to finish it.

Improve Your Grades

Following directions to the letter is very easy; however, some students never seem to realize this. One of the easiest ways to improve your grades is to prepare every assignment exactly as it is assigned. The result will show in your grades.

21-1 WORK TOGETHER, p. 621

Journalizing and posting entries for accrued revenue

1.

Marris Corporation

Work Sheet

For Year Ended December 31, 20 – –

	ACCOUNT TITLE	TRIAL BALANCE		ADJUSTMENTS	
		DEBIT	CREDIT	DEBIT	CREDIT
4	Interest Receivable				
50	Interest Income		1 5 4 5 00		

2., 3.

GENERAL JOURNAL   PAGE 14

	DATE	ACCOUNT TITLE	DOC. NO.	POST. REF.	DEBIT	CREDIT	
1							1
2							2
3							3
4							4
5							5
6							6
7							7
8							8

4.

GENERAL JOURNAL   PAGE 15

	DATE	ACCOUNT TITLE	DOC. NO.	POST. REF.	DEBIT	CREDIT	
1							1
2							2
3							3
4							4

5.

CASH RECEIPTS JOURNAL

				1	2	3	4	5	6	7
				GENERAL		ACCOUNTS RECEIVABLE CREDIT	SALES CREDIT	SALES TAX PAYABLE CREDIT	SALES DISCOUNT DEBIT	CASH DEBIT
DATE	ACCOUNT TITLE	DOC. NO.	POST. REF.	DEBIT	CREDIT					
1										
2										
3										
4										
5										
6										
7										
8										
9										
10										
11										
12										
13										
14										
15										
16										
17										
18										
19										
20										
21										
22										
23										
24										

21-1 WORK TOGETHER (concluded)

2., 3., 4., 5.   **GENERAL LEDGER**

ACCOUNT Notes Receivable   ACCOUNT NO. 1115

DATE	ITEM	POST. REF.	DEBIT	CREDIT	BALANCE DEBIT	BALANCE CREDIT
Nov. 16		G11	4 0 0 0 00		4 0 0 0 00	

ACCOUNT Interest Receivable   ACCOUNT NO. 1120

DATE	ITEM	POST. REF.	DEBIT	CREDIT	BALANCE DEBIT	BALANCE CREDIT

ACCOUNT Income Summary   ACCOUNT NO. 3120

DATE	ITEM	POST. REF.	DEBIT	CREDIT	BALANCE DEBIT	BALANCE CREDIT

ACCOUNT Interest Income   ACCOUNT NO. 7110

DATE	ITEM	POST. REF.	DEBIT	CREDIT	BALANCE DEBIT	BALANCE CREDIT
Dec. 31		CR15		1 5 00		1 5 4 5 00

Journalizing and posting entries for accrued revenue

1.

ExMark, Inc.

Work Sheet

For Year Ended December 31, 20 – –

	ACCOUNT TITLE	TRIAL BALANCE		ADJUSTMENTS	
		DEBIT	CREDIT	DEBIT	CREDIT
4	Interest Receivable				
50	Interest Income		6 9 2 00		

2., 3.

GENERAL JOURNAL   PAGE 14

	DATE	ACCOUNT TITLE	DOC. NO.	POST. REF.	DEBIT	CREDIT	
1							1
2							2
3							3
4							4
5							5
6							6
7							7
8							8

4.

GENERAL JOURNAL   PAGE 15

	DATE	ACCOUNT TITLE	DOC. NO.	POST. REF.	DEBIT	CREDIT	
1							1
2							2
3							3
4							4

21-1 ON YOUR OWN (continued)

5.

CASH RECEIPTS JOURNAL

PAGE 19

					1 GENERAL DEBIT	2 GENERAL CREDIT	3 ACCOUNTS RECEIVABLE CREDIT	4 SALES CREDIT	5 SALES TAX PAYABLE CREDIT	6 SALES DISCOUNT DEBIT	7 CASH DEBIT
DATE	ACCOUNT TITLE	DOC. NO.	POST. REF.								

2., 3., 4., 5.   **GENERAL LEDGER**

ACCOUNT Notes Receivable   ACCOUNT NO. 1115

DATE		ITEM	POST. REF.	DEBIT	CREDIT	BALANCE DEBIT	BALANCE CREDIT
Dec.	1		G11	6 0 0 0 00		6 0 0 0 00	

ACCOUNT Interest Receivable   ACCOUNT NO. 1120

DATE		ITEM	POST. REF.	DEBIT	CREDIT	BALANCE DEBIT	BALANCE CREDIT

ACCOUNT Income Summary   ACCOUNT NO. 3120

DATE		ITEM	POST. REF.	DEBIT	CREDIT	BALANCE DEBIT	BALANCE CREDIT

ACCOUNT Interest Income   ACCOUNT NO. 7110

DATE		ITEM	POST. REF.	DEBIT	CREDIT	BALANCE DEBIT	BALANCE CREDIT
Dec.	31		CR15		8 7 50		6 9 2 00

Name _____ Date _____ Class _____

Journalizing and posting entries for accrued expenses

1.

Powers Corporation

Work Sheet

For Year Ended December 31, 20 – –

	ACCOUNT TITLE	TRIAL BALANCE		ADJUSTMENTS	
		1 DEBIT	2 CREDIT	3 DEBIT	4 CREDIT
15	Interest Payable				
51	Interest Expense	8 4 7 7 00			

2., 3.

GENERAL JOURNAL PAGE 14

	DATE	ACCOUNT TITLE	DOC. NO.	POST. REF.	DEBIT	CREDIT	
1							1
2							2
3							3
4							4
5							5
6							6
7							7
8							8

4.

GENERAL JOURNAL PAGE 15

	DATE	ACCOUNT TITLE	DOC. NO.	POST. REF.	DEBIT	CREDIT	
1							1
2							2
3							3
4							4

5.

CASH PAYMENTS JOURNAL

PAGE 25

								GENERAL		ACCOUNTS PAYABLE DEBIT	PURCHASES DISCOUNT CREDIT	CASH CREDIT
DATE	ACCOUNT TITLE	CK. NO.	POST. REF.	DEBIT		CREDIT						
				1		2			3	4		5
1												
2												
3												
4												
5												
6												
7												
8												
9												
10												
11												
12												
13												
14												
15												
16												
17												
18												
19												
20												
21												
22												
23												
24												

21-2 WORK TOGETHER (concluded)

2., 3., 4., 5.   **GENERAL LEDGER**

ACCOUNT Notes Payable   ACCOUNT NO. 2105

DATE	ITEM	POST. REF.	DEBIT	CREDIT	BALANCE DEBIT	BALANCE CREDIT
Dec. 1		CR13		2 0 0 0 00		2 0 0 0 00

ACCOUNT Interest Payable   ACCOUNT NO. 2110

DATE	ITEM	POST. REF.	DEBIT	CREDIT	BALANCE DEBIT	BALANCE CREDIT

ACCOUNT Income Summary   ACCOUNT NO. 3120

DATE	ITEM	POST. REF.	DEBIT	CREDIT	BALANCE DEBIT	BALANCE CREDIT

ACCOUNT Interest Expense   ACCOUNT NO. 8105

DATE	ITEM	POST. REF.	DEBIT	CREDIT	BALANCE DEBIT	BALANCE CREDIT
Dec. 31		CP19	1 6 0 00		8 4 7 7 00	

Journalizing and posting entries for accrued expenses

1.

Latham Industries

Work Sheet

For Year Ended December 31, 20 – –

		1	2	3	4
	ACCOUNT TITLE	TRIAL BALANCE		ADJUSTMENTS	
		DEBIT	CREDIT	DEBIT	CREDIT
15	Interest Payable				
51	Interest Expense	4 70 8 25			

2., 3.

GENERAL JOURNAL   PAGE 14

	DATE	ACCOUNT TITLE	DOC. NO.	POST. REF.	DEBIT	CREDIT	
1							1
2							2
3							3
4							4
5							5
6							6
7							7
8							8

4.

GENERAL JOURNAL   PAGE 15

	DATE	ACCOUNT TITLE	DOC. NO.	POST. REF.	DEBIT	CREDIT	
1							1
2							2
3							3
4							4

21-2 ON YOUR OWN (continued)

5.

CASH PAYMENTS JOURNAL

PAGE 30

DATE	ACCOUNT TITLE	CK. NO.	POST. REF.	GENERAL DEBIT	GENERAL CREDIT	ACCOUNTS PAYABLE DEBIT	PURCHASES DISCOUNT CREDIT	CASH CREDIT

2., 3., 4., 5.   **GENERAL LEDGER**

ACCOUNT Notes Payable   ACCOUNT NO. 2105

DATE	ITEM	POST. REF.	DEBIT	CREDIT	BALANCE DEBIT	BALANCE CREDIT
Oct. 17		CR9		5 0 0 0 00		5 0 0 0 00

ACCOUNT Interest Payable   ACCOUNT NO. 2110

DATE	ITEM	POST. REF.	DEBIT	CREDIT	BALANCE DEBIT	BALANCE CREDIT

ACCOUNT Income Summary   ACCOUNT NO. 3120

DATE	ITEM	POST. REF.	DEBIT	CREDIT	BALANCE DEBIT	BALANCE CREDIT

ACCOUNT Interest Expense   ACCOUNT NO. 8105

DATE	ITEM	POST. REF.	DEBIT	CREDIT	BALANCE DEBIT	BALANCE CREDIT
Dec. 31		CP24	5 0 00		4 7 0 8 25	

21-1 APPLICATION PROBLEM, p. 629

Journalizing and posting entries for accrued revenue

1.

Velma Parts Company

Work Sheet

For Year Ended December 31, 20 – –

	ACCOUNT TITLE	TRIAL BALANCE		ADJUSTMENTS	
		DEBIT	CREDIT	DEBIT	CREDIT
4	Interest Receivable				
50	Interest Income		1 9 6 7 50		

2., 3.

GENERAL JOURNAL   PAGE 14

	DATE	ACCOUNT TITLE	DOC. NO.	POST. REF.	DEBIT	CREDIT	
1							1
2							2
3							3
4							4
5							5
6							6
7							7
8							8

4.

GENERAL JOURNAL   PAGE 15

	DATE	ACCOUNT TITLE	DOC. NO.	POST. REF.	DEBIT	CREDIT	
1							1
2							2
3							3
4							4

5.

CASH RECEIPTS JOURNAL

PAGE 8

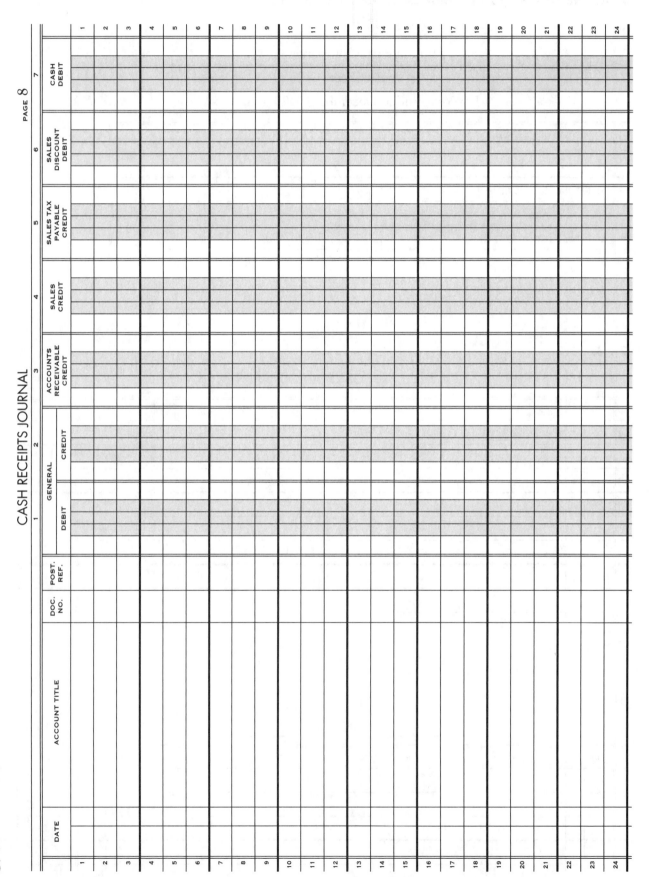

	DATE	ACCOUNT TITLE	DOC. NO.	POST. REF.	GENERAL DEBIT	GENERAL CREDIT	ACCOUNTS RECEIVABLE CREDIT	SALES CREDIT	SALES TAX PAYABLE CREDIT	SALES DISCOUNT DEBIT	CASH DEBIT	
					1	2	3	4	5	6	7	
1												1
2												2
3												3
4												4
5												5
6												6
7												7
8												8
9												9
10												10
11												11
12												12
13												13
14												14
15												15
16												16
17												17
18												18
19												19
20												20
21												21
22												22
23												23
24												24

21-1 APPLICATION PROBLEM (concluded)

2., 3., 4., 5.   **GENERAL LEDGER**

ACCOUNT Notes Receivable   ACCOUNT NO. 1115

DATE		ITEM	POST. REF.	DEBIT	CREDIT	BALANCE DEBIT	BALANCE CREDIT
Nov.	6		G11	8 1 0 0 00		8 1 0 0 00	

ACCOUNT Interest Receivable   ACCOUNT NO. 1120

DATE	ITEM	POST. REF.	DEBIT	CREDIT	BALANCE DEBIT	BALANCE CREDIT

ACCOUNT Income Summary   ACCOUNT NO. 3120

DATE	ITEM	POST. REF.	DEBIT	CREDIT	BALANCE DEBIT	BALANCE CREDIT

ACCOUNT Interest Income   ACCOUNT NO. 7110

DATE		ITEM	POST. REF.	DEBIT	CREDIT	BALANCE DEBIT	BALANCE CREDIT
Dec.	31		CR18		2 5 00		1 9 6 7 50

APPLICATION PROBLEM, p. 629

Journalizing and posting entries for accrued expenses

1.

Delmar Plumbing Supply

Work Sheet

For Year Ended December 31, 20 – –

	ACCOUNT TITLE	TRIAL BALANCE		ADJUSTMENTS	
		1 DEBIT	**2** CREDIT	**3** DEBIT	**4** CREDIT
15	Interest Payable				
51	Interest Expense	8 4 8 9 00			

2., 3.

GENERAL JOURNAL   PAGE 14

	DATE	ACCOUNT TITLE	DOC. NO.	POST. REF.	DEBIT	CREDIT	
1							1
2							2
3							3
4							4
5							5
6							6
7							7
8							8

4.

GENERAL JOURNAL   PAGE 15

	DATE	ACCOUNT TITLE	DOC. NO.	POST. REF.	DEBIT	CREDIT	
1							1
2							2
3							3
4							4

21-2 **APPLICATION PROBLEM (continued)**

5.

CASH PAYMENTS JOURNAL

PAGE 27

DATE	ACCOUNT TITLE	CK. NO.	POST. REF.	GENERAL DEBIT	GENERAL CREDIT	ACCOUNTS PAYABLE DEBIT	PURCHASES DISCOUNT CREDIT	CASH CREDIT
				1	2	3	4	5

2., 3., 4., 5.   **GENERAL LEDGER**

ACCOUNT Notes Payable   ACCOUNT NO. 2105

DATE		ITEM	POST. REF.	DEBIT	CREDIT	BALANCE DEBIT	BALANCE CREDIT
Dec.	1		CR12		12 0 0 0 00		12 0 0 0 00

ACCOUNT Interest Payable   ACCOUNT NO. 2110

DATE		ITEM	POST. REF.	DEBIT	CREDIT	BALANCE DEBIT	BALANCE CREDIT

ACCOUNT Income Summary   ACCOUNT NO. 3120

DATE		ITEM	POST. REF.	DEBIT	CREDIT	BALANCE DEBIT	BALANCE CREDIT

ACCOUNT Interest Expense   ACCOUNT NO. 8105

DATE		ITEM	POST. REF.	DEBIT	CREDIT	BALANCE DEBIT	BALANCE CREDIT
Dec.	31		CP21	1 6 0 00		8 4 8 9 00	

21-3 **APPLICATION PROBLEM, pp. 629, 630**

Journalizing and posting entries for accrued expenses

1.

Patti's Dress Shop

Work Sheet

For Year Ended December 31, 20 – –

	ACCOUNT TITLE	TRIAL BALANCE		ADJUSTMENTS	
		DEBIT	CREDIT	DEBIT	CREDIT
15	Interest Payable				
51	Interest Expense	2 8 9 9 00			

2.

GENERAL JOURNAL   PAGE 16

	DATE	ACCOUNT TITLE	DOC. NO.	POST. REF.	DEBIT	CREDIT	
1							1
2							2
3							3
4							4
5							5
6							6
7							7
8							8

GENERAL JOURNAL   PAGE 17

	DATE	ACCOUNT TITLE	DOC. NO.	POST. REF.	DEBIT	CREDIT	
1							1
2							2
3							3
4							4

3.

CASH PAYMENTS JOURNAL

PAGE 23

DATE	ACCOUNT TITLE	CK. NO.	POST. REF.	GENERAL DEBIT	GENERAL CREDIT	ACCOUNTS PAYABLE DEBIT	PURCHASES DISCOUNT CREDIT	CASH CREDIT
								1
								2
								3
								4
								5
								6
								7
								8
								9
								10
								11
								12
								13
								14
								15
								16
								17
								18
								19
								20
								21
								22
								23
								24

21-3 APPLICATION PROBLEM (concluded)

2., 3.   **GENERAL LEDGER**

ACCOUNT Notes Payable   ACCOUNT NO. 2105

DATE	ITEM	POST. REF.	DEBIT	CREDIT	BALANCE DEBIT	BALANCE CREDIT
Oct. 14		CR11		10 0 0 0 00		10 0 0 0 00

ACCOUNT Interest Payable   ACCOUNT NO. 2110

DATE	ITEM	POST. REF.	DEBIT	CREDIT	BALANCE DEBIT	BALANCE CREDIT

ACCOUNT Income Summary   ACCOUNT NO. 3120

DATE	ITEM	POST. REF.	DEBIT	CREDIT	BALANCE DEBIT	BALANCE CREDIT

ACCOUNT Interest Expense   ACCOUNT NO. 8105

DATE	ITEM	POST. REF.	DEBIT	CREDIT	BALANCE DEBIT	BALANCE CREDIT
Dec. 31		CP19	8 0 00		2 8 9 9 00	

MASTERY PROBLEM, p. 630

Journalizing and posting entries for accrued interest revenue and expenses

1.

Youngblood, Inc.

Work Sheet

For Year Ended December 31, 20X1

	ACCOUNT TITLE	TRIAL BALANCE		ADJUSTMENTS	
		DEBIT	CREDIT	DEBIT	CREDIT
4	Interest Receivable				
15	Interest Payable				
50	Interest Income		1 6 6 7 00		
51	Interest Expense	2 7 3 2 00			

2., 3.

GENERAL JOURNAL   PAGE 15

	DATE	ACCOUNT TITLE	DOC. NO.	POST. REF.	DEBIT	CREDIT	
1							1
2							2
3							3
4							4
5							5
6							6
7							7
8							8
9							9
10							10
11							11

4.

GENERAL JOURNAL   PAGE 16

	DATE	ACCOUNT TITLE	DOC. NO.	POST. REF.	DEBIT	CREDIT	
1							1
2							2
3							3
4							4
5							5

21-4 MASTERY PROBLEM (continued)

5.

CASH RECEIPTS JOURNAL

PAGE 16

DATE	ACCOUNT TITLE	DOC. NO.	POST. REF.	GENERAL DEBIT	GENERAL CREDIT	ACCOUNTS RECEIVABLE CREDIT	SALES CREDIT	SALES TAX PAYABLE CREDIT	SALES DISCOUNT DEBIT	CASH DEBIT
				1	2	3	4	5	6	7

6.

CASH PAYMENTS JOURNAL

PAGE 28

DATE	ACCOUNT TITLE	CK. NO.	POST. REF.	GENERAL DEBIT	GENERAL CREDIT	ACCOUNTS PAYABLE DEBIT	PURCHASES DISCOUNT CREDIT	CASH CREDIT
				1	2	3	4	5

2., 3., 4., 5., 6.   **GENERAL LEDGER**

ACCOUNT Notes Receivable   ACCOUNT NO. 1115

DATE	ITEM	POST. REF.	DEBIT	CREDIT	BALANCE DEBIT	BALANCE CREDIT
Nov. 11		G12	9 0 0 00		9 0 0 00	

ACCOUNT Interest Receivable   ACCOUNT NO. 1120

DATE	ITEM	POST. REF.	DEBIT	CREDIT	BALANCE DEBIT	BALANCE CREDIT

ACCOUNT Notes Payable   ACCOUNT NO. 2105

DATE	ITEM	POST. REF.	DEBIT	CREDIT	BALANCE DEBIT	BALANCE CREDIT
Dec. 6		CR12		7 2 0 0 00		7 2 0 0 00

ACCOUNT Interest Payable   ACCOUNT NO. 2110

DATE	ITEM	POST. REF.	DEBIT	CREDIT	BALANCE DEBIT	BALANCE CREDIT

21-4 MASTERY PROBLEM (concluded)

2., 3., 4., 5., 6.   **GENERAL LEDGER**

ACCOUNT Income Summary   ACCOUNT NO. 3120

DATE	ITEM	POST. REF.	DEBIT	CREDIT	BALANCE DEBIT	BALANCE CREDIT

ACCOUNT Interest Income   ACCOUNT NO. 7110

DATE	ITEM	POST. REF.	DEBIT	CREDIT	BALANCE DEBIT	BALANCE CREDIT
Dec. 31		CR14		3 2 00		1 6 6 7 00

ACCOUNT Interest Expense   ACCOUNT NO. 8105

DATE	ITEM	POST. REF.	DEBIT	CREDIT	BALANCE DEBIT	BALANCE CREDIT
Dec. 31		CP21	8 7 50		2 7 3 2 00	

Journalizing and posting entries for accrued interest revenue and expenses

1.

Blackwell Corporation

Work Sheet

For Year Ended December 31, 20X1

		1	2	3	4
	ACCOUNT TITLE	TRIAL BALANCE		ADJUSTMENTS	
		DEBIT	CREDIT	DEBIT	CREDIT
4	Interest Receivable				
15	Interest Payable				
50	Interest Income		1 8 9 7 00		
51	Interest Expense	1 6 4 8 00			

2.

GENERAL JOURNAL

	DATE	ACCOUNT TITLE	DOC. NO.	POST. REF.	DEBIT	CREDIT	
1							1
2							2
3							3
4							4
5							5
6							6
7							7
8							8
9							9
10							10
11							11

GENERAL JOURNAL

	DATE	ACCOUNT TITLE	DOC. NO.	POST. REF.	DEBIT	CREDIT	
1							1
2							2
3							3
4							4
5							5

21-5 CHALLENGE PROBLEM (continued)

3.

GENERAL JOURNAL

PAGE 18

DATE	ACCOUNT TITLE	DOC. NO.	POST. REF.	DEBIT	CREDIT

CASH PAYMENTS JOURNAL

PAGE 15

					1	2	3	4	5
DATE	ACCOUNT TITLE	CK. NO.	POST. REF.		GENERAL DEBIT	GENERAL CREDIT	ACCOUNTS PAYABLE DEBIT	PURCHASES DISCOUNT CREDIT	CASH CREDIT

2., 3.   **GENERAL LEDGER**

ACCOUNT Notes Receivable   ACCOUNT NO. 1115

DATE		ITEM	POST. REF.	DEBIT	CREDIT	BALANCE	
						DEBIT	CREDIT
Dec.	8		G14	9 0 0 00		9 0 0 00	

ACCOUNT Interest Receivable   ACCOUNT NO. 1120

DATE	ITEM	POST. REF.	DEBIT	CREDIT	BALANCE	
					DEBIT	CREDIT

ACCOUNT Notes Payable   ACCOUNT NO. 2105

DATE		ITEM	POST. REF.	DEBIT	CREDIT	BALANCE	
						DEBIT	CREDIT
Dec.	15		CR12		10 0 0 0 00		10 0 0 0 00

ACCOUNT Interest Payable   ACCOUNT NO. 2110

DATE	ITEM	POST. REF.	DEBIT	CREDIT	BALANCE	
					DEBIT	CREDIT

21-5 CHALLENGE PROBLEM (concluded)

2., 3.   **GENERAL LEDGER**

ACCOUNT Income Summary   ACCOUNT NO. 3120

DATE	ITEM	POST. REF.	DEBIT	CREDIT	BALANCE DEBIT	BALANCE CREDIT

ACCOUNT Interest Income   ACCOUNT NO. 7110

DATE	ITEM	POST. REF.	DEBIT	CREDIT	BALANCE DEBIT	BALANCE CREDIT
Dec. 31		CR12		85 00		1 897 00

ACCOUNT Interest Expense   ACCOUNT NO. 8105

DATE	ITEM	POST. REF.	DEBIT	CREDIT	BALANCE DEBIT	BALANCE CREDIT
Dec. 31		CP12	100 00		1 648 00	

	Perfect Score	Your Score
Name		
Identifying Accounting Concepts and Practices for End-of-Fiscal-Period Work	20 Pts.	
Analyzing End-of-Fiscal-Period Entries for a Corporation	34 Pts.	
Total	54 Pts.	

Study Guide 22

Part One—Identifying Accounting Concepts and Practices for End-of-Fiscal-Period Work

Directions: Place a *T* for True or an *F* for False in the Answers column to show whether each of the following statements is true or false.

Answers

1. Financial statements are prepared using a completed work sheet. (p. 636) 1. _____

2. Businesses use work sheets to plan adjustments and provide information needed to prepare financial statements. (p. 636) 2. _____

3. All accounts that need to be brought up to date are adjusted after financial statements are prepared. (p. 637) 3. _____

4. To adjust the interest income earned during the current fiscal period but not yet received, the Interest Receivable account is debited. (p. 638) 4. _____

5. To bring the Supplies account up to date, the balance of supplies needs to be decreased by the cost of supplies used during the year. (p. 638) 5. _____

6. Federal income tax is an expense of a corporation. (p. 639) 6. _____

7. The tax rate for federal income tax varies depending on the amount of net income earned. (p. 639) 7. _____

8. Corporations with less than $50,000 net income pay smaller tax rates than corporations with larger net incomes. (p. 640) 8. _____

9. When the total of a work sheet's Income Statement Credit column is larger than the total of the Income Statement Debit column, the difference represents net loss of the business. (p. 641) 9. _____

10. A work sheet's Balance Sheet columns are used to calculate net income after federal income tax. (p. 641) 10. _____

11. The balance of Capital Stock is recorded in the Income Statement columns of a work sheet. (p. 642) 11. _____

12. A corporation's preparation of financial statements to report the financial progress during a fiscal period is an application of the Accounting Period Cycle concept. (p. 646) 12. _____

13. To calculate the component percentage of cost of merchandise sold, divide net sales by cost of merchandise sold. (p. 647) 13. _____

14. A statement of stockholders' equity contains two major sections: capital stock and retained earnings. (p. 649) 14. _____

15. The book value of an asset is reported on a balance sheet by listing two amounts: the balance of the asset account and the balance of the asset's contra account. (p. 651) 15. _____

16. An example of a long-term liability is Mortgage Payable. (p. 651) 16. _____

17. A business can use the amount of working capital to provide a convenient relative measurement from year to year. (p. 652) 17. _____

18. Closing entries for a corporation are made from information in a balance sheet. (p. 655)

19. Dividends increase the earnings retained by a corporation. (p. 657)

20. A reversing entry is desirable if an adjusting entry creates a balance in an asset or a liability account. (p. 658)

Part Two—Analyzing End-of-Fiscal-Period Entries for a Corporation

Directions: For each closing or reversing entry described, decide which accounts are debited and credited. Print the letter identifying your choice in the proper Answers columns. (Accounts are listed in alphabetical order.)

Account Titles	Transactions	Answers Debit	Credit
A. Cash Short and Over	**1–2.** Closing entry for the sales account. (p. 655)	1. _____	2. _____
B. Depreciation Expense —Store Equipment	**3–4.** Closing entry for purchases discount. (p. 655)	3. _____	4. _____
C. Dividends	**5–6.** Closing entry for the purchases returns and allowances account. (p. 655)	5. _____	6. _____
D. Dividends Payable	**7–8.** Closing entry for the gain on plant assets account. (p. 655)	7. _____	8. _____
E. Federal Income Tax Expense	**9–10.** Closing entry for the interest income account. (p. 655)	9. _____	10. _____
F. Federal Income Tax Payable	**11–12.** Closing entry for the sales discount account. (p. 656)	11. _____	12. _____
G. Gain on Plant Assets	**13–14.** Closing entry for the purchases account. (p. 656)	13. _____	14. _____
H. Income Summary	**15–16.** Closing entry for the cash short and over account (cash is short). (p. 656)	15. _____	16. _____
I. Insurance Expense	**17–18.** Closing entry for the cash short and over account (cash is over). (p. 656)	17. _____	18. _____
J. Interest Expense	**19–20.** Closing entry for the depreciation expense—store equipment account. (p. 656)	19. _____	20. _____
K. Interest Income	**21–22.** Closing entry for the federal income tax expense account. (p. 656)	21. _____	22. _____
L. Interest Payable	**23–24.** Closing entry for the income summary account (net income). (p. 657)	23. _____	24. _____
M. Interest Receivable	**25–26.** Closing entry for the income summary account (net loss). (p. 657)	25. _____	26. _____
N. Loss on Plant Assets	**27–28.** Closing entry for the dividends account. (p. 657)	27. _____	28. _____
O. Purchases	**29–30.** Reversing entry for the accrued interest income account. (p. 658)	29. _____	30. _____
P. Purchases Discount	**31–32.** Reversing entry for the accrued interest expense. (p. 658)	31. _____	32. _____
Q. Purchases Returns and Allowances	**33–34.** Reversing entry for the federal income tax payable account. (p. 658)	33. _____	34. _____
R. Retained Earnings			
S. Sales			
T. Sales Discount			

Study Skills

Estimating Math Answers

Being able to estimate math answers quickly is advantageous for everyone. When you go shopping, do you know approximately how much your bill is going to be before you check out? Before you work out a math problem at school, do you know about what the answer should be?

Make a Good Guess
Being able to estimate answers will help you at school. Suppose you want to average 10 grades ranging from 90 to 100. You should be able to estimate that the total of the 10 grades should be about 950, and the average should be about 95. If your answer is 70 when you calculate the average, you know immediately that the answer is not sensible.

Avoid Errors Using Decimal Places
Students sometimes place a decimal in the wrong place in the answer to a math problem. This is an error that you will not make if you know approximately how much the answer should be before you begin figuring.

This may sound surprising, but students sometimes make an error similar to the following. The teacher asks what is 10 percent of $100, and the student answers $1,000.

Any student who takes a few seconds to think about the problem will know immediately that the answer is smaller, not larger, than the original $100. By estimating the answer first, you can avoid making what appears to be a ridiculous error.

Dependence on the Calculator
The pocket calculator is a wonderful device. It can save you a great amount of time when you must do a math problem. However, you must not let yourself become so dependent on a calculator that you make errors simply because you do not estimate answers.

A Sensible Approach
Being able to estimate math answers can help you every day. Before you begin calculating, ask yourself what a sensible answer would be. If the final answer is not reasonably close to your estimate, you have very likely made an error. A little practice can save you money when you shop and improve your grades at school.

[This page left blank intentionally.]

Preparing a work sheet for a corporation

1., 2.

Webster Corporation
Work Sheet
For Year Ended December 31, 20 – –

	ACCOUNT TITLE	TRIAL BALANCE DEBIT	TRIAL BALANCE CREDIT	ADJUSTMENTS DEBIT	ADJUSTMENTS CREDIT	INCOME STATEMENT DEBIT	INCOME STATEMENT CREDIT	BALANCE SHEET DEBIT	BALANCE SHEET CREDIT
1	Cash	90 05 2 23							
2	Petty Cash	3 00 00							
3	Notes Receivable	10 95 2 00							
4	Interest Receivable								
5	Accounts Receivable	70 09 4 10							
6	Allowance for Uncoll. Accts.		44 64						
7	Merchandise Inventory	64 31 6 30							
8	Supplies	2 55 2 08							
9	Prepaid Insurance	9 07 1 60							
10	Office Equipment	27 94 0 00							
11	Accum. Depr.—Office Equip.		6 73 5 00						
12	Store Equipment	22 19 9 20							
13	Accum. Depr.—Store Equip.		6 35 7 40						
14	Notes Payable		14 40 0 00						
15	Interest Payable								
16	Accounts Payable		60 11 6 18						
17	Employee Inc. Tax Payable		1 65 2 40						
18	Federal Inc. Tax Payable								
19	Social Security Tax Payable		1 54 9 19						
20	Medicare Tax Payable		3 57 51						
21	Sales Tax Payable		6 65 2 60						
22	Unemploy. Tax Pay.—Fed.		33 44						
23	Unemploy. Tax Pay.—State		2 25 72						
24	Health Ins. Premiums Pay.		70 2 60						
25	Dividends Payable		10 80 0 00						
26	Capital Stock		100 00 0 00						
27	Retained Earnings		59 24 1 54						
28	Dividends	43 20 0 00							
29	Income Summary								
30	Sales		1075 86 8 30						
31	Sales Discount	2 02 0 80							
32	Sales Ret. and Allowances	8 34 7 20							

Total of Income Statement Credit column _____

Less total of Income Statement Debit column
    before federal income tax _____

Equals Net Income before Federal Income Tax _____

22-1 WORK TOGETHER (concluded)

Webster Corporation
Work Sheet (continued)
For Year Ended December 31, 20- -

	ACCOUNT TITLE	TRIAL BALANCE DEBIT	TRIAL BALANCE CREDIT	ADJUSTMENTS DEBIT	ADJUSTMENTS CREDIT	INCOME STATEMENT DEBIT	INCOME STATEMENT CREDIT	BALANCE SHEET DEBIT	BALANCE SHEET CREDIT	
33	Purchases	737 464 80								33
34	Purchases Discount		5 483 60							34
35	Purchases Ret. and Allow.		2 716 14							35
36	Advertising Expense	15 947 00								36
37	Cash Short and Over	9 15								37
38	Credit Card Fee Expense	10 066 94								38
39	Depr. Exp.—Office Equip.									39
40	Depr. Exp.—Store Equip.									40
41	Insurance Expense									41
42	Miscellaneous Expense	8 682 20								42
43	Payroll Taxes Expense	14 966 00								43
44	Rent Expense	28 915 00								44
45	Repair Expense	3 485 00								45
46	Salary Expense	158 964 00								46
47	Supplies Expense									47
48	Uncollectible Accounts Exp.									48
49	Utilities Expense	26 661 00								49
50	Gain on Plant Assets		1 100 00							50
51	Interest Income		894 48							51
52	Interest Expense	2 186 14								52
53	Loss on Plant Assets	2 480 00								53
54	Federal Income Tax Expense	19 300 00								54
55		1353 940 74	1353 940 74							55
56	Net Inc. after Fed. Inc. Tax									56
57										57
58										58
59										59
60										60
61										61
62										62

Net Income before Taxes	×	Tax Rate	=	Federal Income Tax Amount
$50,000.00	×	15%	=	
Plus 25,000.00	×	25%	=	
Plus	×	34%	=	
Plus	×	39%	=	
Total				

Preparing a work sheet for a corporation

1., 2.

Osborn Corporation

Work Sheet

For Year Ended December 31, 20 – –

	TRIAL BALANCE		ADJUSTMENTS		INCOME STATEMENT		BALANCE SHEET	
ACCOUNT TITLE	DEBIT	CREDIT	DEBIT	CREDIT	DEBIT	CREDIT	DEBIT	CREDIT
1 Cash	6 848 00							
2 Petty Cash	300 00							
3 Notes Receivable	8 000 00							
4 Interest Receivable								
5 Accounts Receivable	82 483 22							
6 Allowance for Uncoll. Accts.		280 00						
7 Merchandise Inventory	195 884 25							
8 Supplies	9 218 25							
9 Prepaid Insurance	15 800 00							
10 Office Equipment	35 188 50							
11 Accum. Depr.—Office Equip.		22 188 50						
12 Store Equipment	43 884 25							
13 Accum. Depr.—Store Equip.		28 178 00						
14 Notes Payable		9 000 00						
15 Interest Payable								
16 Accounts Payable		18 489 25						
17 Employee Inc. Tax Payable		2 256 00						
18 Federal Inc. Tax Payable								
19 Social Security Tax Payable		2 121 34						
20 Medicare Tax Payable		512 66						
21 Sales Tax Payable		5 976 00						
22 Unemploy. Tax Pay.—Fed.		45 60						
23 Unemploy. Tax Pay.—State		292 80						
24 Health Ins. Premiums Pay.		672 00						
25 Dividends Payable		5 000 00						
26 Capital Stock		50 000 00						
27 Retained Earnings		54 142 16						
28 Dividends	20 000 00							

Total of Income Statement Credit column _____

Less total of Income Statement Debit column
before federal income tax _____

Equals Net Income before Federal Income Tax _____

22-1 ON YOUR OWN (concluded)

Osborn Corporation
Work Sheet (continued)
For Year Ended December 31, 20 – –

	Account Title	Trial Balance Debit	Trial Balance Credit	Adjustments Debit	Adjustments Credit	Income Statement Debit	Income Statement Credit	Balance Sheet Debit	Balance Sheet Credit	
29	Income Summary									29
30	Sales		2584 4 8 3 25							30
31	Sales Discount	12 4 8 5 28								31
32	Sales Returns and Allow.	22 8 9 4 10								32
33	Purchases	1638 8 1 7 14								33
34	Purchases Discount		7 8 9 1 17							34
35	Purchases Ret. and Allow.		6 1 4 8 20							35
36	Advertising Expense	38 1 1 4 20								36
37	Cash Short and Over	1 5 33								37
38	Credit Card Fee Expense	18 1 2 2 10								38
39	Depr. Exp.—Office Equip.									39
40	Depr. Exp.—Store Equip.									40
41	Insurance Expense									41
42	Miscellaneous Expense	29 4 8 5 25								42
43	Payroll Taxes Expense	32 1 4 8 24								43
44	Rent Expense	54 0 0 0 00								44
45	Repair Expense	12 4 8 7 93								45
46	Salary Expense	421 5 8 4 99								46
47	Supplies Expense									47
48	Uncollectible Accounts Exp.									48
49	Utilities Expense	23 1 9 9 90								49
50	Gain on Plant Assets		2 4 5 8 00							50
51	Interest Income		6 2 5 00							51
52	Interest Expense	1 7 8 0 00								52
53	Loss on Plant Assets	2 0 1 9 00								53
54	Federal Income Tax Expense	76 0 0 0 00								54
55		2800 7 5 9 93	2800 7 5 9 93							55
56	Net Inc. after Fed. Inc. Tax									56
57										57

Net Income before Taxes	×	Tax Rate	=	Federal Income Tax Amount
$ 50,000.00	×	15%	=	
Plus 25,000.00	×	25%	=	
Plus 25,000.00	×	34%	=	
Plus	×	39%	=	
Total				

Preparing an income statement for a corporation

1.

					% OF NET SALES

22-2 WORK TOGETHER (concluded)

1.

										% OF NET SALES

2.

	Acceptable %	Actual %	Positive Result		Recommended Action If Needed
			Yes	No	
Cost of merchandise sold	Not more than 68.0%				
Gross profit on operations	Not less than 32.0%				
Total operating expenses	Not more than 22.0%				
Income from operations	Not less than 10.0%				
Net deduction from other revenue and expenses	Not more than 0.1%				
Net income before federal income tax	Not less than 9.8%				

Preparing an income statement for a corporation

1.

									% OF NET SALES

22-2 ON YOUR OWN (concluded)

1.

		% OF NET SALES

	Acceptable %	Actual %	Positive Result		Recommended Action If Needed
			Yes	No	
Cost of merchandise sold	Not more than 60.0%				
Gross profit on operations	Not less than 40.0%				
Total operating expenses	Not more than 28.0%				
Income from operations	Not less than 12.0%				
Net deduction from other revenue and expenses	Not more than 0.1%				
Net income before federal income tax	Not less than 11.9%				

Preparing a statement of stockholders' equity and balance sheet for a corporation

1.

22-3 **WORK TOGETHER (continued)**

2.

2.

3., 4.

	Acceptable	Actual	Positive Result		Recommended Action If Needed
			Yes	No	
Working capital	Not less than $150,000				
Current ratio	Between 2.0 to 1 and 3.0 to 1				

22-3 ON YOUR OWN, p. 653

Preparing a statement of stockholders' equity and balance sheet for a corporation

1.

2.

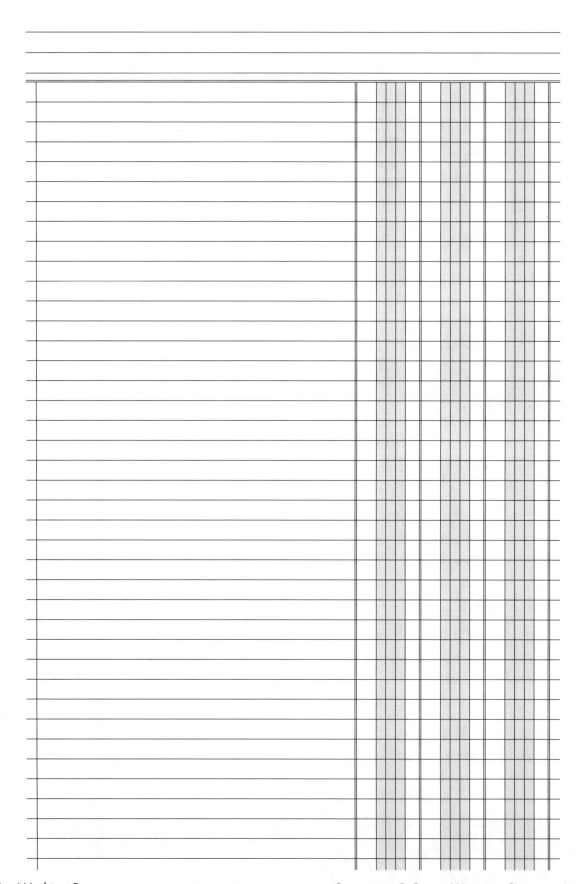

22-3 ON YOUR OWN (concluded)

3., 4.

	Acceptable	Actual	Positive Result		Recommended Action If Needed
			Yes	No	
Working capital	Not less than $100,000				
Current ratio	Between 5.0 to 1 and 6.0 to 1				

Journalizing adjusting, closing, and reversing entries for a corporation

1.

GENERAL JOURNAL

PAGE 15

	DATE	ACCOUNT TITLE	DOC. NO.	POST. REF.	DEBIT	CREDIT	
1							1
2							2
3							3
4							4
5							5
6							6
7							7
8							8
9							9
10							10
11							11
12							12
13							13
14							14
15							15
16							16
17							17
18							18
19							19
20							20
21							21
22							22
23							23
24							24
25							25
26							26
27							27
28							28
29							29
30							30
31							31
32							32

22-4 **WORK TOGETHER (continued)**

2.

		GENERAL JOURNAL				PAGE 16	

	DATE	ACCOUNT TITLE	DOC. NO.	POST. REF.	DEBIT	CREDIT	
1							1
2							2
3							3
4							4
5							5
6							6
7							7
8							8
9							9
10							10
11							11
12							12
13							13
14							14
15							15
16							16
17							17
18							18
19							19
20							20
21							21
22							22
23							23
24							24
25							25
26							26
27							27
28							28
29							29
30							30
31							31
32							32
33							33

3.

GENERAL JOURNAL

	DATE		ACCOUNT TITLE	DOC. NO.	POST. REF.	DEBIT	CREDIT	
1								1
2								2
3								3
4								4
5								5
6								6
7								7
8								8
9								9
10								10
11								11
12								12
13								13
14								14
15								15
16								16
17								17
18								18
19								19
20								20
21								21
22								22
23								23
24								24
25								25
26								26
27								27
28								28
29								29
30								30
31								31
32								32
33								33

Name _____ Date _____ Class _____

22-4 ON YOUR OWN, p. 660

Journalizing adjusting, closing, and reversing entries for a corporation

1.

GENERAL JOURNAL

	DATE	ACCOUNT TITLE	DOC. NO.	POST. REF.	DEBIT	CREDIT	
1							1
2							2
3							3
4							4
5							5
6							6
7							7
8							8
9							9
10							10
11							11
12							12
13							13
14							14
15							15
16							16
17							17
18							18
19							19
20							20
21							21
22							22
23							23
24							24
25							25
26							26
27							27
28							28
29							29
30							30
31							31
32							32

2.

			GENERAL JOURNAL				PAGE 19

	DATE		ACCOUNT TITLE	DOC. NO.	POST. REF.	DEBIT	CREDIT	
1								1
2								2
3								3
4								4
5								5
6								6
7								7
8								8
9								9
10								10
11								11
12								12
13								13
14								14
15								15
16								16
17								17
18								18
19								19
20								20
21								21
22								22
23								23
24								24
25								25
26								26
27								27
28								28
29								29
30								30
31								31
32								32
33								33

22-4 **ON YOUR OWN (concluded)**

3.

GENERAL JOURNAL   PAGE 20

	DATE	ACCOUNT TITLE	DOC. NO.	POST. REF.	DEBIT	CREDIT	
1							1
2							2
3							3
4							4
5							5
6							6
7							7
8							8
9							9
10							10
11							11
12							12
13							13
14							14
15							15
16							16
17							17
18							18
19							19
20							20
21							21
22							22
23							23
24							24
25							25
26							26
27							27
28							28
29							29
30							30
31							31
32							32
33							33

Preparing a work sheet for a corporation

1., 2.

Donovan Lumber Corporation

Work Sheet

For Year Ended December 31, 20 – –

| | TRIAL BALANCE | | ADJUSTMENTS | | INCOME STATEMENT | | BALANCE SHEET | |
ACCOUNT TITLE	DEBIT	CREDIT	DEBIT	CREDIT	DEBIT	CREDIT	DEBIT	CREDIT
1 Cash	3 8 4 8 58							
2 Petty Cash	3 0 0 00							
3 Notes Receivable	5 8 4 8 80							
4 Interest Receivable								
5 Accounts Receivable	57 1 8 7 80							
6 Allowance for Uncoll. Accts.		6 6 48						
7 Merchandise Inventory	78 8 5 8 00							
8 Supplies	4 9 8 7 70							
9 Prepaid Insurance	8 9 4 8 00							
10 Office Equipment	26 4 8 8 00							
11 Accum. Depr.—Office Equip.		8 4 8 8 00						
12 Store Equipment	17 4 9 8 00							
13 Accum. Depr.—Store Equip.		4 8 7 1 40						
14 Notes Payable		30 0 0 0 00						
15 Interest Payable								
16 Accounts Payable		8 3 7 2 80						
17 Employee Inc. Tax Payable		1 4 8 6 30						
18 Federal Inc. Tax Payable								
19 Social Security Tax Payable		1 2 0 9 81						
20 Medicare Tax Payable		2 7 9 19						
21 Sales Tax Payable		2 8 4 7 00						
22 Unemploy. Tax Pay.—Fed.		2 9 25						
23 Unemploy. Tax Pay.—State		1 9 5 00						
24 Health Ins. Premiums Pay.		3 4 8 80						
25 Dividends Payable		5 0 0 0 00						
26 Capital Stock		50 0 0 0 00						
27 Retained Earnings		30 8 2 3 18						
28 Dividends	20 0 0 0 00							
29 Income Summary								
30 Sales		983 8 3 7 20						
31 Sales Discount	1 8 9 4 50							
32 Sales Ret. and Allowances	4 5 8 3 50							

2. Total of Income Statement Credit column _____

Less total of Income Statement Debit column

before federal income tax _____

Equals Net Income before Federal Income Tax _____

22-1 APPLICATION PROBLEM (concluded)

Donovan Lumber Corporation
Work Sheet (continued)
For Year Ended December 31, 20 – –

	ACCOUNT TITLE	TRIAL BALANCE DEBIT	TRIAL BALANCE CREDIT	ADJUSTMENTS DEBIT	ADJUSTMENTS CREDIT	INCOME STATEMENT DEBIT	INCOME STATEMENT CREDIT	BALANCE SHEET DEBIT	BALANCE SHEET CREDIT
33	Purchases	697 318 50							
34	Purchases Discount		4 215 50						
35	Purchases Ret. and Allow.		1 848 47						
36	Advertising Expense	9 483 80							
37	Cash Short and Over	10 20							
38	Credit Card Fee Expense	8 482 90							
39	Depr. Exp.—Office Equip.								
40	Depr. Exp.—Store Equip.								
41	Insurance Expense								
42	Miscellaneous Expense	9 184 80							
43	Payroll Taxes Expense	12 848 00							
44	Rent Expense	15 000 00							
45	Repair Expense	4 104 80							
46	Salary Expense	125 483 20							
47	Supplies Expense								
48	Uncollectible Accounts Exp.								
49	Utilities Expense	7 158 90							
50	Gain on Plant Assets		7 15 00						
51	Interest Income		2 27 00						
52	Interest Expense	3 158 40							
53	Loss on Plant Assets	1 84 00							
54	Federal Income Tax Expense	12 000 00							
55		1134 860 38	1134 860 38						
56	Net Inc. after Fed. Inc. Tax								
57									
58									
59									
60									
61									
62									
63									
64									

2.

Net Income before Taxes	×	Tax Rate	=	Federal Income Tax Amount
$50,000.00	×	15%	=	
Plus	×	25%	=	
Plus	×	34%	=	
Plus	×	39%	=	
Total				

APPLICATION PROBLEM, p. 662

Preparing an income statement for a corporation

1., 2.

					% OF NET SALES

22-2 APPLICATION PROBLEM (concluded)

1., 2.

		% OF NET SALES

3.

	Acceptable %	Actual %	Positive Result		Recommended Action If Needed
			Yes	No	
Cost of merchandise sold	Not more than 70.0%				
Gross profit on operations	Not less than 30.0%				
Total operating expenses	Not more than 25.0%				
Income from operations	Not less than 5.0%				
Net deduction from other revenue and expenses	Not more than 0.1%				
Net income before federal income tax	Not less than 4.9%				

APPLICATION PROBLEM, p. 663

Preparing a statement of stockholders' equity and balance sheet for a corporation

1.

22-3 APPLICATION PROBLEM (continued)

2.

2.

3., 4.

	Acceptable	Actual	Positive Result		Recommended Action If Needed
			Yes	No	
Working capital	Not less than $100,000				
Current ratio	Between 3.0 to 1 and 3.5 to 1				

22-4 APPLICATION PROBLEM, p. 663

Journalizing adjusting, closing, and reversing entries for a corporation

1.

GENERAL JOURNAL   PAGE 15

	DATE		ACCOUNT TITLE	DOC. NO.	POST. REF.	DEBIT	CREDIT	
1								1
2								2
3								3
4								4
5								5
6								6
7								7
8								8
9								9
10								10
11								11
12								12
13								13
14								14
15								15
16								16
17								17
18								18
19								19
20								20
21								21
22								22
23								23
24								24
25								25
26								26
27								27
28								28
29								29
30								30
31								31
32								32

2.

GENERAL JOURNAL

	DATE	ACCOUNT TITLE	DOC. NO.	POST. REF.	DEBIT	CREDIT	
1							1
2							2
3							3
4							4
5							5
6							6
7							7
8							8
9							9
10							10
11							11
12							12
13							13
14							14
15							15
16							16
17							17
18							18
19							19
20							20
21							21
22							22
23							23
24							24
25							25
26							26
27							27
28							28
29							29
30							30
31							31
32							32
33							33

22-4 **APPLICATION PROBLEM (concluded)**

3.

GENERAL JOURNAL   PAGE 17

	DATE	ACCOUNT TITLE	DOC. NO.	POST. REF.	DEBIT	CREDIT	
1							1
2							2
3							3
4							4
5							5
6							6
7							7
8							8
9							9
10							10
11							11
12							12
13							13
14							14
15							15
16							16
17							17
18							18
19							19
20							20
21							21
22							22
23							23
24							24
25							25
26							26
27							27
28							28
29							29
30							30
31							31
32							32
33							33

MASTERY PROBLEM, pp. 663, 664

Preparing a work sheet, financial statement, and end-of-fiscal-period entries for a corporation

1.

Benford Corporation
Work Sheet
For Year Ended December 31, 20 - -

	ACCOUNT TITLE	TRIAL BALANCE DEBIT	TRIAL BALANCE CREDIT	ADJUSTMENTS DEBIT	ADJUSTMENTS CREDIT	INCOME STATEMENT DEBIT	INCOME STATEMENT CREDIT	BALANCE SHEET DEBIT	BALANCE SHEET CREDIT
1	Cash	2 5 1 8 25							
2	Petty Cash	5 0 0 00							
3	Notes Receivable	4 0 0 0 00							
4	Interest Receivable								
5	Accounts Receivable	12 5 8 4 8 25							
6	Allowance for Uncoll. Accts.	1 6 0 00							
7	Merchandise Inventory	288 3 1 8 08							
8	Supplies	6 4 8 1 28							
9	Prepaid Insurance	1 4 0 0 0 00							
10	Office Equipment	2 9 1 4 8 22							
11	Accum. Depr.—Office Equip.		8 7 1 0 00						
12	Store Equipment	2 7 1 5 8 00							
13	Accum. Depr.—Store Equip.		18 1 6 0 00						
14	Notes Payable		25 0 0 0 00						
15	Interest Payable								
16	Accounts Payable		32 1 5 8 29						
17	Employee Inc. Tax Payable		2 4 5 8 80						
18	Federal Inc. Tax Payable								
19	Social Security Tax Payable		2 1 2 1 31						
20	Medicare Tax Payable		5 1 2 69						
21	Sales Tax Payable		2 5 1 8 66						
22	Unemploy. Tax Pay.—Fed.		4 5 60						
23	Unemploy. Tax Pay.—State		2 9 2 80						
24	Health Ins. Premiums Pay.		6 7 2 00						
25	Dividends Payable		8 0 0 0 00						
26	Capital Stock		150 0 0 0 00						
27	Retained Earnings		149 1 8 3 00						
28	Dividends	32 0 0 0 00							
29	Income Summary								
30	Sales		2251 8 9 3 17						
31	Sales Discount	5 8 9 4 36							
32	Sales Ret. and Allowances	15 4 8 7 39							

Total of Income Statement Credit column _____
Less total of Income Statement Debit column
     before federal income tax _____
Equals Net Income before Federal Income Tax _____

22-5 MASTERY PROBLEM (continued)

Benford Corporation
Work Sheet (continued)
For Year Ended December 31, 20 – –

	ACCOUNT TITLE	TRIAL BALANCE DEBIT	TRIAL BALANCE CREDIT	ADJUSTMENTS DEBIT	ADJUSTMENTS CREDIT	INCOME STATEMENT DEBIT	INCOME STATEMENT CREDIT	BALANCE SHEET DEBIT	BALANCE SHEET CREDIT
33	Purchases	1498 1 8 3 08							
34	Purchases Discount		13 1 1 8 02						
35	Purchases Ret. and Allow.		6 1 8 4 16						
36	Advertising Expense	16 4 8 6 90							
37	Cash Short and Over	1 6 88							
38	Credit Card Fee Expense	8 4 8 9 33							
39	Depr. Exp.—Office Equip.								
40	Depr. Exp.—Store Equip.								
41	Insurance Expense								
42	Miscellaneous Expense	4 2 1 8 6 30							
43	Payroll Taxes Expense	3 2 1 8 4 02							
44	Rent Expense	4 5 0 0 0 00							
45	Repair Expense	6 1 5 4 99							
46	Salary Expense	421 5 4 8 36							
47	Supplies Expense								
48	Uncollectible Accounts Exp.								
49	Utilities Expense	20 4 4 5 61							
50	Gain on Plant Assets		1 5 4 8 00						
51	Interest Income		6 4 8 00						
52	Interest Expense	3 6 0 0 00							
53	Loss on Plant Assets	2 4 1 5 20							
54	Federal Income Tax Expense	25 0 0 0 00							
55		2673 2 2 4 50	2673 2 2 4 50						
56	Net Inc. after Fed. Inc. Tax								
57									

Net Income before Taxes	×	Tax Rate	=	Federal Income Tax Amount
$50,000.00	×	15%	=	
Plus 25,000.00	×	25%	=	
Plus 25,000.00	×	34%	=	
Plus	×	39%	=	
Total				

2.

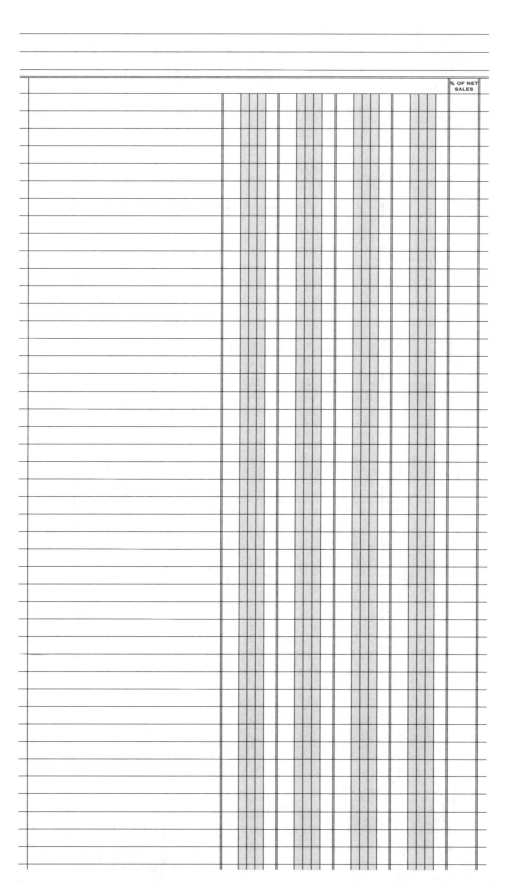

22-5 MASTERY PROBLEM (continued)

3. Income Statement Analysis

	Acceptable %	Actual %	Positive Result		Recommended Action If Needed
			Yes	No	
Cost of merchandise sold	Not more than 70.0%				
Gross profit on operations	Not less than 30.0%				
Total operating expenses	Not more than 25.0%				
Income from operations	Not less than 5.0%				
Net deduction from other revenue and expenses	Not more than 0.1%				
Net income before federal income tax	Not less than 4.9%				

4.

5.

22-5 MASTERY PROBLEM (continued)

6. Balance Sheet Analysis

	Acceptable	Actual	Positive Result		Recommended Action If Needed
			Yes	No	
Working capital	Not less than $150,000				
Current ratio	Between 3.0 to 1 and 4.0 to 1				

7.

GENERAL JOURNAL PAGE 15

	DATE		ACCOUNT TITLE	DOC. NO.	POST. REF.	DEBIT	CREDIT	
1								1
2								2
3								3
4								4
5								5
6								6
7								7
8								8
9								9
10								10
11								11
12								12
13								13
14								14
15								15
16								16
17								17
18								18
19								19
20								20
21								21

8.

GENERAL JOURNAL

PAGE 16

	DATE		ACCOUNT TITLE	DOC. NO.	POST. REF.	DEBIT	CREDIT	
1								1
2								2
3								3
4								4
5								5
6								6
7								7
8								8
9								9
10								10
11								11
12								12
13								13
14								14
15								15
16								16
17								17
18								18
19								19
20								20
21								21
22								22
23								23
24								24
25								25
26								26
27								27
28								28
29								29
30								30
31								31
32								32
33								33

22-5 MASTERY PROBLEM (concluded)

9.

	DATE	ACCOUNT TITLE	DOC. NO.	POST. REF.	DEBIT	CREDIT	
1							1
2							2
3							3
4							4
5							5
6							6
7							7
8							8
9							9
10							10
11							11
12							12
13							13
14							14
15							15
16							16
17							17
18							18
19							19
20							20
21							21
22							22
23							23
24							24
25							25
26							26
27							27
28							28
29							29
30							30
31							31
32							32
33							33
34							34

Analyzing financial strength

1.

Name of Corporation	Working Capital	Current Ratio
1.		
2.		

Calculations:

2.

_____

_____

_____

_____

_____

_____

_____

_____

_____

_____

_____

_____

_____

_____

_____

Name _____ Date _____ Class _____

22-6 CHALLENGE PROBLEM (concluded)

3.

An accounting cycle for a corporation: end-of-fiscal-period work

10., 11., 12.

Sparkle, Inc.
Work Sheet
For Year Ended December 31, 20X4

	ACCOUNT TITLE	TRIAL BALANCE DEBIT	TRIAL BALANCE CREDIT	ADJUSTMENTS DEBIT	ADJUSTMENTS CREDIT	INCOME STATEMENT DEBIT	INCOME STATEMENT CREDIT	BALANCE SHEET DEBIT	BALANCE SHEET CREDIT
1	Cash	8 1 0 0 70							
2	Petty Cash	2 0 0 00							
3	Notes Receivable	3 6 0 0 00							
4	Interest Receivable								
5	Accounts Receivable	7 8 9 4 60							
6	Allowance for Uncoll. Accts.	1 4 6 9 40							
7	Merchandise Inventory	74 1 7 6 95							
8	Supplies	3 0 9 9 05							
9	Prepaid Insurance	8 6 0 00							
10	Office Equipment	2 3 8 3 00							
11	Accum. Depr.—Office Equip.		7 1 6 0 00						
12	Warehouse Equipment	26 1 1 0 00							
13	Accum. Depr.—Warehouse Equip.		7 0 4 0 00						
14	Notes Payable		16 0 0 0 00						
15	Interest Payable								
16	Accounts Payable		14 1 1 2 65						
17	Federal Income Tax Pay.								
18	Employee Income Tax Pay.		3 1 0 00						
19	Social Security Tax Pay.		6 9 1 92						
20	Medicare Tax Payable		1 6 1 82						
21	Sales Tax Payable		6 2 1 0 66						
22	Unemploy. Tax Pay.—Fed.		2 1 53						
23	Unemploy. Tax Pay.—State		1 4 5 29						
24	Health Ins. Premiums Pay.		1 1 0 5 00						
25	Dividends Payable		5 0 0 0 00						
26	Capital Stock		30 0 0 0 00						
27	Retained Earnings		23 8 8 9 20						
28	Dividends	20 0 0 0 00							
29	Income Summary								
30	Sales		779 2 1 0 90						
31	Sales Discount	1 8 8 9 20							

REINFORCEMENT ACTIVITY 3 PART B (continued)

Sparkle, Inc.

Work Sheet (continued)

For Year Ended December 31, 20X4

	ACCOUNT TITLE	TRIAL BALANCE DEBIT	TRIAL BALANCE CREDIT	ADJUSTMENTS DEBIT	ADJUSTMENTS CREDIT	INCOME STATEMENT DEBIT	INCOME STATEMENT CREDIT	BALANCE SHEET DEBIT	BALANCE SHEET CREDIT	
32	Sales Returns and Allow.	6174 80								32
33	Purchases	529022 40								33
34	Purchases Discount		3596 08							34
35	Purchases Returns and Allow.		3236 00							35
36	Advertising Expense	9606 70								36
37	Cash Short and Over	20 09								37
38	Credit Card Fee Expense	14529 40								38
39	Depr. Expense—Office Equip.	24000 00								39
40	Depr. Expense—Ware. Equip.	44000 00								40
41	Insurance Expense									41
42	Miscellaneous Expense	5828 32								42
43	Payroll Taxes Expense	10669 44								43
44	Rent Expense	21000 00								44
45	Repairs Expense	1394 80								45
46	Salary Expense	104878 00								46
47	Supplies Expense									47
48	Uncollectible Accounts Exp.									48
49	Utilities Expense	7236 20								49
50	Gain on Plant Assets		7450 00							50
51	Interest Income		4140 0							51
52	Interest Expense	2750 00								52
53	Loss on Plant Assets	2900 0								53
54	Federal Income Tax Expense	60000 0								54
55		899050 5 05	899050 5 05							55
56	Net Income after Fed. In. Tax									56
57										57

Total of Income Statement Credit column _____

Less total of Income Statement Debit column
before federal income tax _____

Equals Net Income before Federal Income Tax

	Net Income before Taxes	Tax Rate		Federal Income Tax Amount
	$50,000.00	× 15%	=	_____
	_____	× 25%	=	_____
				_____

13.

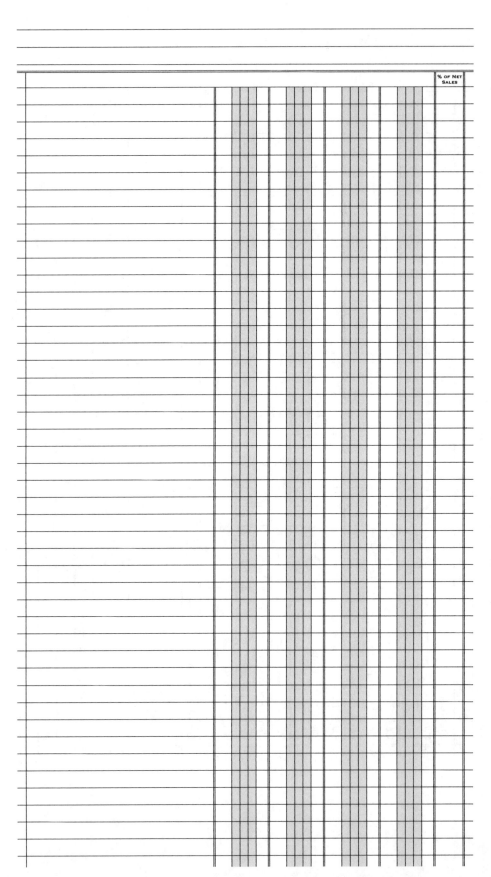

														% OF NET SALES

REINFORCEMENT ACTIVITY 3 PART B (continued)

14.

	Acceptable %	Actual %	Positive Result Yes	Positive Result No	Recommended Action If Needed
Cost of merchandise sold	Not more than 62.0%				
Gross profit on operations	Not less than 38.0%				
Total operating expenses	Not more than 28.0%				
Income from operations	Not less than 10.0%				
Net deductions from other revenue and expenses	Not more than 0.5%				
Net income before federal income tax	Not less than 9.5%				

15.

Net Income after Federal Income Tax	÷	Number of Shares Outstanding	=	Earnings per Share
$	÷		=	$

Market Price per Share	÷	Earnings per Share	=	Price-Earnings Ratio
$	÷	$	=	

16.

REINFORCEMENT ACTIVITY 3 PART B (continued)

17.

18.

		GENERAL JOURNAL				PAGE 13	
	DATE	ACCOUNT TITLE	DOC. NO.	POST. REF.	DEBIT	CREDIT	
1							1
2							2
3							3
4							4
5							5
6							6
7							7
8							8
9							9
10							10
11							11
12							12
13							13
14							14
15							15
16							16
17							17
18							18
19							19
20							20
21							21
22							22
23							23
24							24
25							25
26							26
27							27
28							28
29							29
30							30
31							31
32							32
33							33

REINFORCEMENT ACTIVITY 3 PART B (continued)

19.

GENERAL JOURNAL   PAGE 14

	DATE		ACCOUNT TITLE	DOC. NO.	POST. REF.	DEBIT	CREDIT	
1								1
2								2
3								3
4								4
5								5
6								6
7								7
8								8
9								9
10								10
11								11
12								12
13								13
14								14
15								15
16								16
17								17
18								18
19								19
20								20
21								21
22								22
23								23
24								24
25								25
26								26
27								27
28								28
29								29
30								30
31								31
32								32
33								33

20.

ACCOUNT TITLE	DEBIT	CREDIT

REINFORCEMENT ACTIVITY 3 PART B (concluded)

21.

GENERAL JOURNAL

PAGE 15

	DATE		ACCOUNT TITLE	DOC. NO.	POST. REF.	DEBIT	CREDIT	
1								1
2								2
3								3
4								4
5								5
6								6
7								7
8								8
9								9
10								10
11								11
12								12
13								13
14								14
15								15
16								16
17								17
18								18
19								19
20								20
21								21
22								22
23								23
24								24
25								25
26								26
27								27
28								28
29								29
30								30
31								31
32								32
33								33

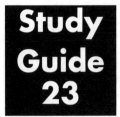

Study Guide 23

Name	Perfect Score	Your Score
Identifying Accounting Terms	8 Pts.	
Identifying Accounting Concepts and Practices	12 Pts.	
Analyzing Partnership Transactions	27 Pts.	
Total	47 Pts.	

Part One—Identifying Accounting Terms

Directions: Select the one term in Column I that best fits each definition in Column II. Print the letter identifying your choice in the Answers column.

Column I

A. distribution of net income statement

B. owners' equity statement

C. partner

D. partnership

E. partnership agreement

F. liquidation of a partnership

G. limited liability partnership (LLP)

H. realization

Column II

1. A business in which two or more persons combine their assets and skills. (p. 674)

2. Each member of a partnership. (p. 674)

3. A written agreement setting forth the conditions under which a partnership is to operate. (p. 675)

4. A partnership financial statement showing net income or loss distribution to partners. (p. 680)

5. A financial statement that summarizes the changes in owners' equity during a fiscal period. (p. 682)

6. The process of paying a partnership's liabilities and distributing remaining assets to the partners. (p. 686)

7. Cash received from the sale of assets during liquidation of a partnership. (p. 686)

8. A partnership that combines the advantages of the partnership and the corporation, while avoiding their disadvantages. (p. 688)

Answers

1. _____

2. _____

3. _____

4. _____

5. _____

6. _____

7. _____

8. _____

Part Two—Identifying Accounting Concepts and Practices

Directions: Place a *T* for True or an *F* for False in the Answers column to show whether each of the following statements is true or false.

1. In a partnership, it is not necessary to separate reports and financial records of the business from the personal records of the partners. (p. 674)

   1. _____

2. During a fiscal period, partners may take assets out of the partnership in anticipation of the net income for the period. (p. 677)

   2. _____

3. Withdrawals reduce the amount of a business's capital. (p. 677)

   3. _____

4. The drawing accounts have normal credit balances. (p. 677)

   4. _____

5. Withdrawals are normally recorded in separate accounts so that the total amounts are easily determined for each accounting period. (p. 677)

   5. _____

6. A partnership's net income or net loss must be divided equally between the partners. (p. 680)

   6. _____

7. The owners' equity statement enables business owners to determine if owners' equity is increasing or decreasing and what is causing the change. (p. 682)

   7. _____

8. When a partnership goes out of business, any remaining cash is distributed to the partners according to each partner's total equity. (p. 686)

   8. _____

9. Noncash assets cannot be sold for more than the recorded book value. (p. 687)

   9. _____

10. A credit balance in the Loss and Gain on Realization account indicates a gain on realization. (p. 689)

    10. _____

11. The distribution for loss or gain on realization is based on the method of distributing net income or net loss as stated in the partnership agreement. (p. 689)

    11. _____

12. If there is a loss on realization, each partner's capital account is debited for the partner's share of the loss. (p. 689)

    12. _____

Part Two—Analyzing Partnership Transactions

Directions: Analyze each of the following transactions into debit and credit parts. Print the letter identifying your choices in the proper Answers column. Determine in which journal each of the transactions is to be recorded.

G—General Journal   CP—Cash Payments Journal   CR—Cash Receipts Journal

Account Titles	Transactions	Journal	Answers Debit	Credit
A. Accounts Payable	**1–2–3.** Partners Katrina Welsh and Bruce Collinson each contribute cash and office equipment to the partnership. (p. 676)	1. _____	2. _____	3. _____
B. Accumulated Depreciation—Office Equipment	**4–5–6.** Bruce Collinson withdraws cash from the business for personal use. (p. 677)	4. _____	5. _____	6. _____
C. Bruce Collinson, Capital	**7–8–9.** Katrina Welsh withdraws office equipment for personal use. (p. 678)	7. _____	8. _____	9. _____
D. Bruce Collinson, Drawing	**10–11–12.** The partnership is liquidated, and the office equipment, costing $32,000 and having a book value of $20,000, is sold for $22,500. (p. 686)	10. _____	11. _____	12. _____
E. Cash				
F. Katrina Welsh, Capital	**13–14–15.** The partnership is liquidated, and the supplies valued at $800 are sold for $650. (p. 687)	13. _____	14. _____	15. _____
G. Katrina Welsh, Drawing	**16–17–18.** The partnership is liquidated, and cash is paid to all creditors for the amounts owed. (p. 688)	16. _____	17. _____	18. _____
H. Loss and Gain on Realization	**19–20–21.** A gain on realization is distributed to the partners. (p. 689)	19. _____	20. _____	21. _____
I. Office Equipment	**22–23–24.** A loss on realization is distributed to the partners. (p. 689)	22. _____	23. _____	24. _____
J. Purchases	**25–26–27.** After liquidation, the remaining cash is distributed to the partners. (p. 689)	25. _____	26. _____	27. _____
K. Supplies				

23-1 WORK TOGETHER, p. 679

Journalizing partners' investments and withdrawals

1.

CASH RECEIPTS JOURNAL

2.

CASH PAYMENTS JOURNAL

PAGE 1

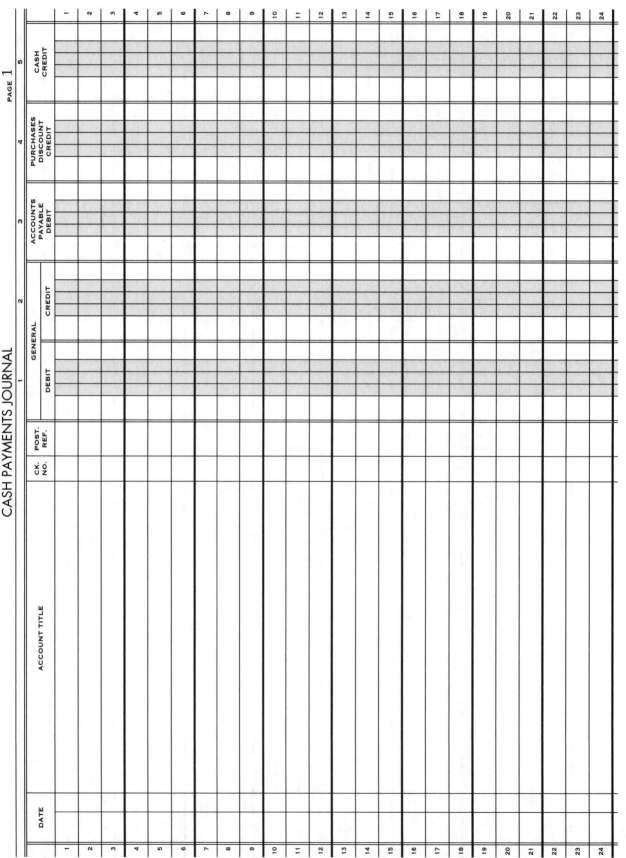

					1 GENERAL DEBIT	2 GENERAL CREDIT	3 ACCOUNTS PAYABLE DEBIT	4 PURCHASES DISCOUNT CREDIT	5 CASH CREDIT	
	DATE	ACCOUNT TITLE	CK. NO.	POST. REF.						
1										1
2										2
3										3
4										4
5										5
6										6
7										7
8										8
9										9
10										10
11										11
12										12
13										13
14										14
15										15
16										16
17										17
18										18
19										19
20										20
21										21
22										22
23										23
24										24

23-1 **WORK TOGETHER (concluded)**

2.

GENERAL JOURNAL

PAGE 3

	DATE	ACCOUNT TITLE	DOC. NO.	POST. REF.	DEBIT	CREDIT	
1							1
2							2
3							3
4							4
5							5
6							6
7							7
8							8
9							9
10							10
11							11
12							12
13							13
14							14
15							15
16							16
17							17
18							18
19							19
20							20
21							21
22							22
23							23
24							24
25							25
26							26
27							27
28							28
29							29
30							30
31							31
32							32
33							33

Journalizing partners' investments and withdrawals

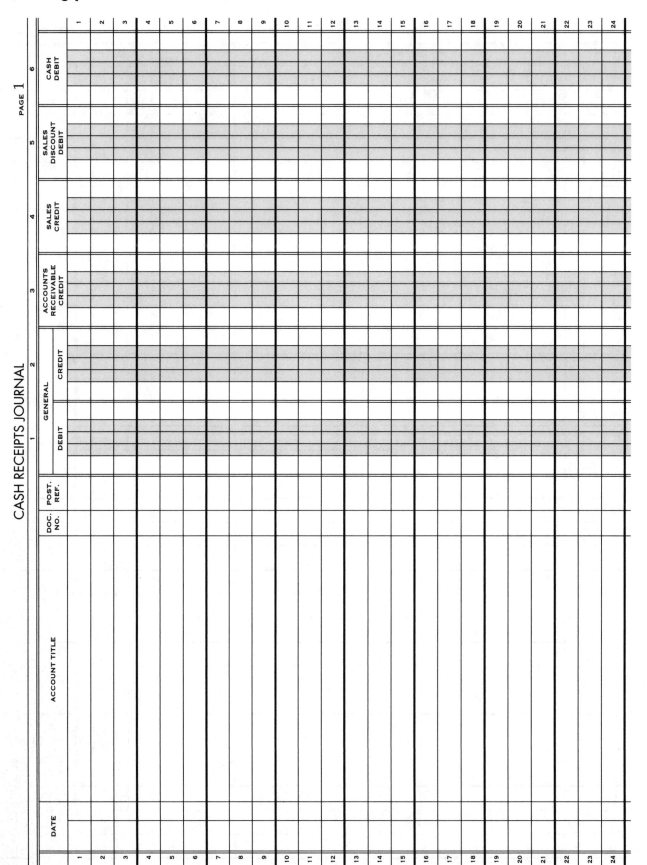

1.

CASH RECEIPTS JOURNAL

PAGE 1

	DATE	ACCOUNT TITLE	DOC. NO.	POST. REF.	GENERAL DEBIT	GENERAL CREDIT	ACCOUNTS RECEIVABLE CREDIT	SALES CREDIT	SALES DISCOUNT DEBIT	CASH DEBIT	
1											1
2											2
3											3
4											4
5											5
6											6
7											7
8											8
9											9
10											10
11											11
12											12
13											13
14											14
15											15
16											16
17											17
18											18
19											19
20											20
21											21
22											22
23											23
24											24

23-1 ON YOUR OWN (continued)

2.

CASH PAYMENTS JOURNAL

PAGE 1

| | | | GENERAL | | ACCOUNTS PAYABLE DEBIT | PURCHASES DISCOUNT CREDIT | CASH CREDIT |
DATE	ACCOUNT TITLE	CK. NO.	POST. REF.	DEBIT 1	CREDIT 2	3	4	5

2.

GENERAL JOURNAL PAGE 9

	DATE	ACCOUNT TITLE	DOC. NO.	POST. REF.	DEBIT	CREDIT	
1							1
2							2
3							3
4							4
5							5
6							6
7							7
8							8
9							9
10							10
11							11
12							12
13							13
14							14
15							15
16							16
17							17
18							18
19							19
20							20
21							21
22							22
23							23
24							24
25							25
26							26
27							27
28							28
29							29
30							30
31							31
32							32
33							33

23-2 **WORK TOGETHER, p. 685**

Preparing distribution of net income and owners' equity statements

1.

_____

_____

2.

_____

_____

Preparing distribution of net income and owners' equity statements

1.

2.

23-3 WORK TOGETHER, p. 690

Liquidation of a partnership

Cash	$12,500.00
Supplies	1,250.00
Office Equipment	15,000.00
Accumulated Depreciation—Office Equipment	8,250.00
Truck	25,500.00
Accumulated Depreciation—Truck	18,300.00
Accounts Payable	1,250.00
Jason Edson, Capital	13,450.00
Peggy Karam, Capital	13,000.00

1.

GENERAL JOURNAL   PAGE 4

	DATE	ACCOUNT TITLE	DOC. NO.	POST. REF.	DEBIT	CREDIT	
1							1
2							2
3							3
4							4
5							5
6							6
7							7
8							8
9							9
10							10
11							11
12							12
13							13
14							14
15							15
16							16
17							17
18							18
19							19
20							20

1.

CASH RECEIPTS JOURNAL

PAGE 6

| | | | | GENERAL | | ACCOUNTS RECEIVABLE CREDIT | SALES CREDIT | SALES DISCOUNT DEBIT | CASH DEBIT | |
DATE	ACCOUNT TITLE	DOC. NO.	POST. REF.	DEBIT	CREDIT					
				1	2	3	4	5	6	1
										2
										3
										4
										5
										6
										7
										8
										9
										10
										11

1.

CASH PAYMENTS JOURNAL

PAGE 8

| | | | | GENERAL | | ACCOUNTS PAYABLE DEBIT | CASH CREDIT | |
DATE	ACCOUNT TITLE	CK. NO.	POST. REF.	DEBIT	CREDIT			
				1	2	3	4	1
								2
								3
								4
								5
								6
								7
								8

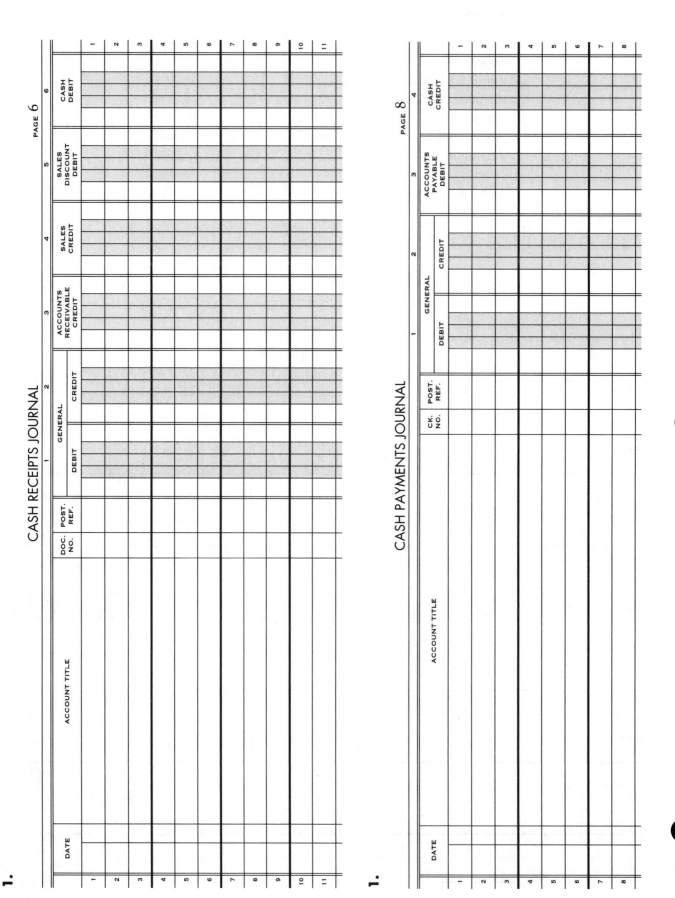

23-3 ON YOUR OWN, p. 690

Liquidation of a partnership

Cash	$17,500.00
Supplies	1,500.00
Office Equipment	10,000.00
Accumulated Depreciation—Office Equipment	8,000.00
Truck	35,000.00
Accumulated Depreciation—Truck	30,000.00
Accounts Payable	8,000.00
Daska Madura, Capital	13,000.00
Lawrence Neary, Capital	5,000.00

1.

GENERAL JOURNAL   PAGE 5

	DATE	ACCOUNT TITLE	DOC. NO.	POST. REF.	DEBIT	CREDIT	
1							1
2							2
3							3
4							4
5							5
6							6
7							7
8							8
9							9
10							10
11							11
12							12
13							13
14							14
15							15
16							16
17							17
18							18
19							19
20							20

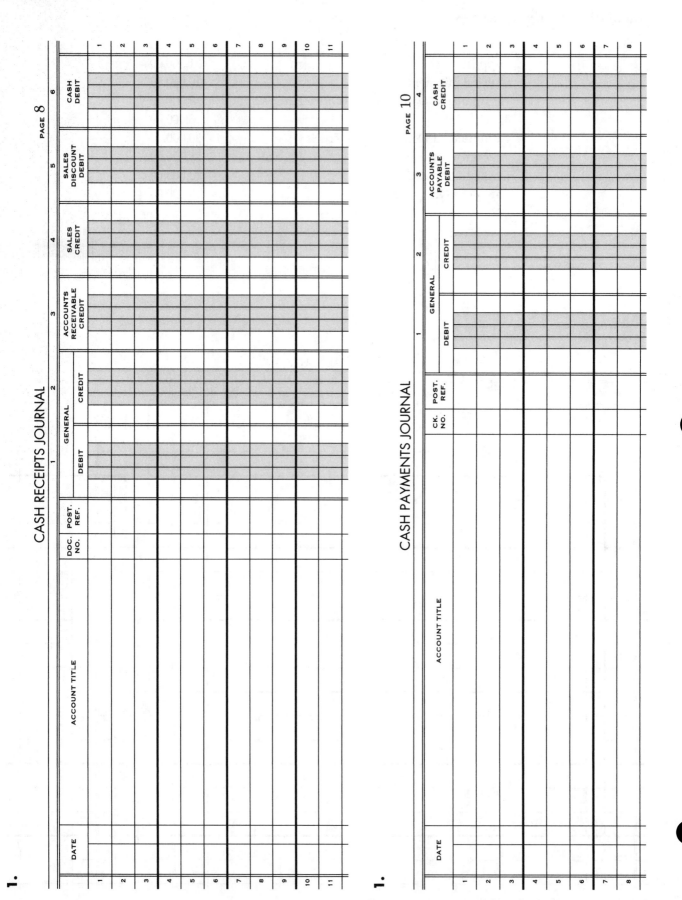

1.

CASH RECEIPTS JOURNAL

PAGE 8

	DATE	ACCOUNT TITLE	DOC. NO.	POST. REF.	GENERAL		ACCOUNTS RECEIVABLE CREDIT	SALES CREDIT	SALES DISCOUNT DEBIT	CASH DEBIT	
					DEBIT	CREDIT					
					1	2	3	4	5	6	
1											1
2											2
3											3
4											4
5											5
6											6
7											7
8											8
9											9
10											10
11											11

1.

CASH PAYMENTS JOURNAL

PAGE 10

	DATE	ACCOUNT TITLE	CK. NO.	POST. REF.	GENERAL		ACCOUNTS PAYABLE DEBIT	CASH CREDIT	
					DEBIT	CREDIT			
					1	2	3	4	
1									1
2									2
3									3
4									4
5									5
6									6
7									7
8									8

23-1 APPLICATION PROBLEM, p. 692

Journalizing partners' investments and withdrawals

1.

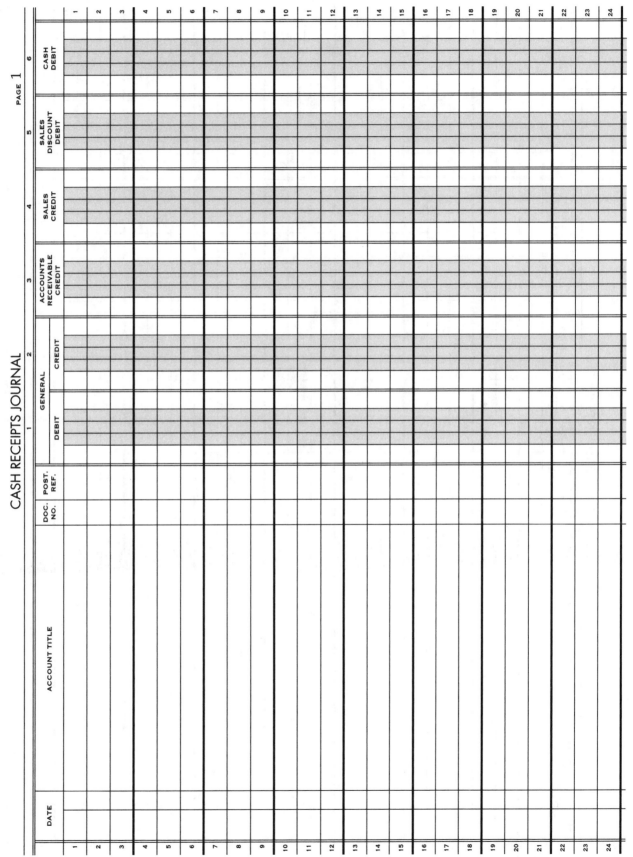

CASH RECEIPTS JOURNAL

2.

CASH PAYMENTS JOURNAL

PAGE 5

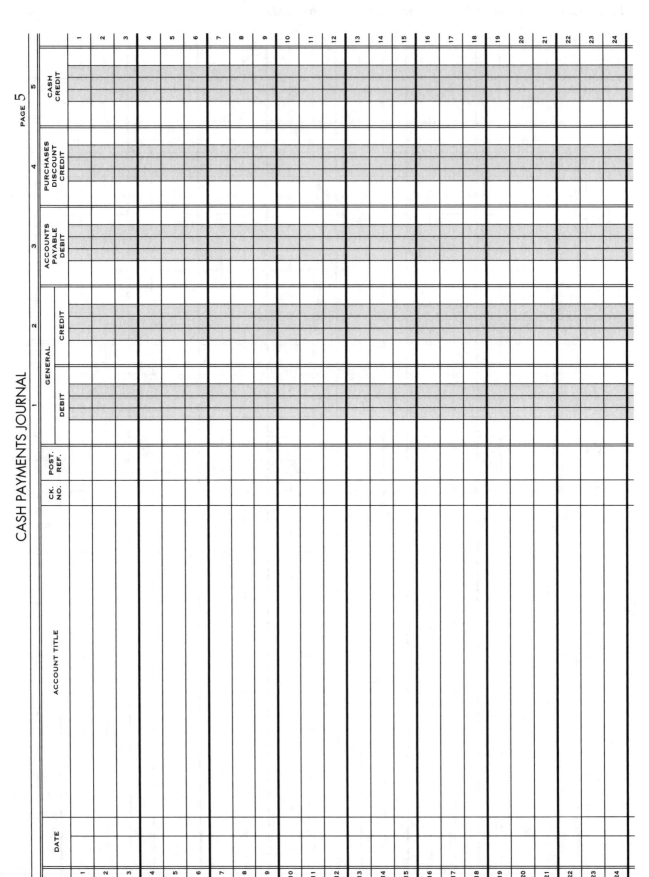

	DATE	ACCOUNT TITLE	CK. NO.	POST. REF.	GENERAL DEBIT	GENERAL CREDIT	ACCOUNTS PAYABLE DEBIT	PURCHASES DISCOUNT CREDIT	CASH CREDIT	
1										1
2										2
3										3
4										4
5										5
6										6
7										7
8										8
9										9
10										10
11										11
12										12
13										13
14										14
15										15
16										16
17										17
18										18
19										19
20										20
21										21
22										22
23										23
24										24

23-1 **APPLICATION PROBLEM (concluded)**

2.

GENERAL JOURNAL   PAGE 12

	DATE	ACCOUNT TITLE	DOC. NO.	POST. REF.	DEBIT	CREDIT	
1							1
2							2
3							3
4							4
5							5
6							6
7							7
8							8
9							9
10							10
11							11
12							12
13							13
14							14
15							15
16							16
17							17
18							18
19							19
20							20
21							21
22							22
23							23
24							24
25							25
26							26
27							27
28							28
29							29
30							30
31							31
32							32
33							33

Preparing distribution of net income and owners' equity statements (net income)

1.

23-2 APPLICATION PROBLEM (concluded)

2.

Preparing an owners' equity statement (net loss)

1.

23-4 APPLICATION PROBLEM, p. 693

Liquidating a partnership

1.

GENERAL JOURNAL   PAGE 7

	DATE	ACCOUNT TITLE	DOC. NO.	POST. REF.	DEBIT	CREDIT	
1							1
2							2
3							3
4							4
5							5
6							6
7							7
8							8
9							9
10							10
11							11
12							12
13							13
14							14
15							15
16							16
17							17
18							18
19							19
20							20
21							21
22							22
23							23
24							24
25							25
26							26
27							27
28							28
29							29
30							30
31							31
32							32

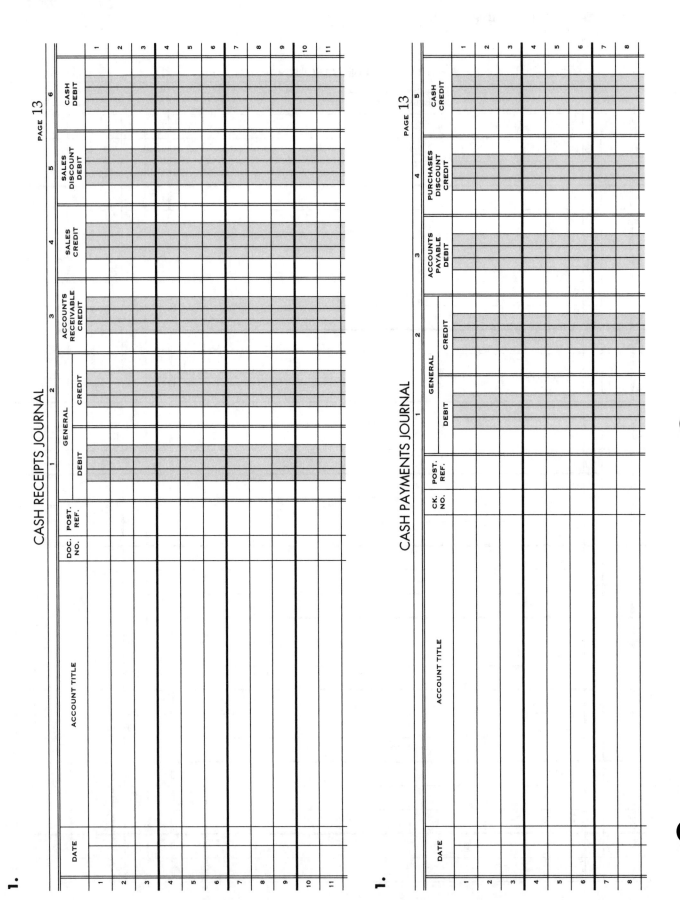

1.

CASH RECEIPTS JOURNAL

PAGE 13

1.

CASH PAYMENTS JOURNAL

PAGE 13

23-5 MASTERY PROBLEM, pp. 694, 695

Recording partners' investments and withdrawals, preparing financial statements, and liquidating a partnership

1., 5.

CASH RECEIPTS JOURNAL

PAGE 13

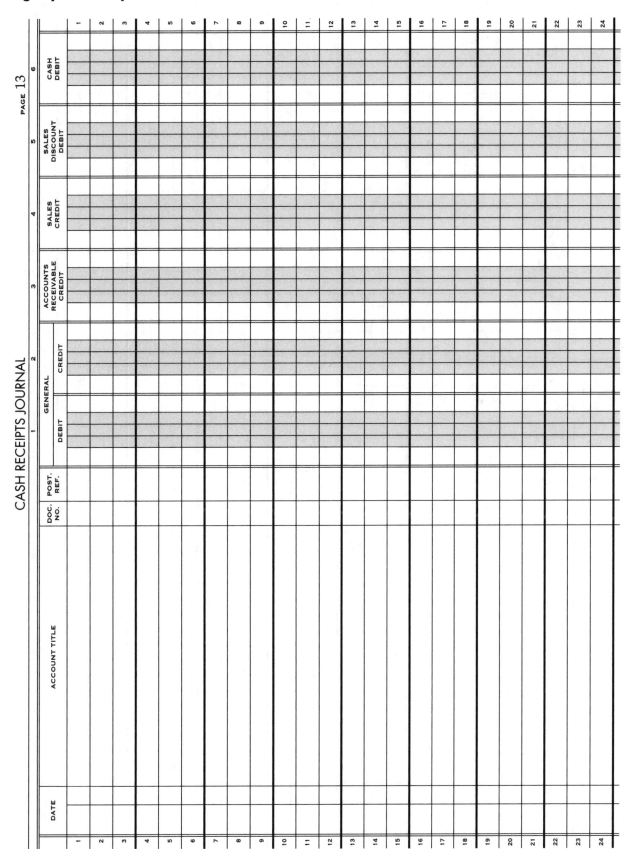

2., 5.

CASH PAYMENTS JOURNAL

DATE	ACCOUNT TITLE	CK. NO.	POST. REF.	GENERAL DEBIT	GENERAL CREDIT	ACCOUNTS PAYABLE DEBIT	PURCHASES DISCOUNT CREDIT	CASH CREDIT	
									1
									2
									3
									4
									5
									6
									7
									8
									9
									10
									11
									12
									13
									14
									15
									16
									17
									18
									19
									20
									21
									22
									23
									24

23-5 **MASTERY PROBLEM (continued)**

2., 5.

GENERAL JOURNAL

	DATE	ACCOUNT TITLE	DOC. NO.	POST. REF.	DEBIT	CREDIT	
1							1
2							2
3							3
4							4
5							5
6							6
7							7
8							8
9							9
10							10
11							11
12							12
13							13
14							14
15							15
16							16
17							17
18							18
19							19
20							20
21							21
22							22
23							23
24							24
25							25
26							26
27							27
28							28
29							29
30							30
31							31
32							32
33							33

3.

23-5 **MASTERY PROBLEM (concluded)**

4.

Preparing a distribution of net income statement and owners' equity statement (unequal distribution of net loss; additional investment)

1.

23-6 CHALLENGE PROBLEM (concluded)

2.

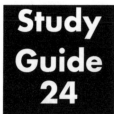

Study Guide 24

Name	Perfect Score	Your Score
Identifying Accounting Terms	10 Pts.	
Analyzing International and Internet Sales	10 Pts.	
Analyzing Accounts Affected by International and Internet Transactions	12 Pts.	
Total	32 Pts.	

Part One—Identifying Accounting Terms

Directions: Select the one term in Column I that best fits each definition in Column II. Print the letter identifying your choice in the Answers column.

Column I	Column II	Answers
A. bill of lading	**1.** Goods or services shipped out of a seller's home country to a foreign country. (p. 702)	1. _____
B. commercial invoice	**2.** Goods or services bought from a foreign country and brought into a buyer's home country. (p. 702)	2. _____
C. contract of sale	**3.** A document that details all the terms agreed to by seller and buyer for a sales transaction. (p. 703)	3. _____
D. draft	**4.** A letter issued by a bank guaranteeing that a named individual or business will be paid a specified amount provided stated conditions are met. (p. 703)	4. _____
E. exports		
F. imports	**5.** A receipt signed by the authorized agent of a transportation company for merchandise received that also serves as a contract for the delivery of the merchandise. (p. 704)	5. _____
G. letter of credit		
H. sight draft	**6.** A statement prepared by the seller of merchandise addressed to the buyer showing a detailed listing and description of merchandise sold, including price and terms. (p. 704)	6. _____
I. time draft		
J. trade acceptance	**7.** A written, signed, and dated order from one party ordering another party, usually a bank, to pay money to a third party. (p. 704)	7. _____
	8. A draft payable on sight when the holder presents it for payment. (p. 704)	8. _____
	9. A draft that is payable at a fixed or determinable future time after it is accepted. (p. 707)	9. _____
	10. A form signed by a buyer at the time of a sale of merchandise in which the buyer promises to pay the seller a specified sum of money, usually at a stated time in the future. (p. 708)	10. _____

Part Two—Analyzing International and Internet Sales

Directions: Place a *T* for True or an *F* for False in the Answers column to show whether each of the following statements is true or false.

Answers

1. International sales are just as simple as domestic sales. (p. 702)   1. _____

2. All transactions in the United States are covered by the same universal commercial laws and the same accounting standards. (p. 703)   2. _____

3. The risk of uncollected amounts is increased with international sales. (p. 703)   3. _____

4. A draft is sometimes referred to as a bank exchange. (p. 704)   4. _____

5. Sales taxes are normally paid only on sales to the final consumer. (p. 706)   5. _____

6. A seller generally has much more assurance of receiving payment from a buyer than from a bank. (p. 708)   6. _____

7. Most businesses use trade acceptances in international sales. (p. 708)   7. _____

8. Companies that sell on the Internet must be able to accept credit card sales. (p. 710)   8. _____

9. The terminal summary is used as the source document for Internet sales. (p. 710)   9. _____

10. Credit card sales are not considered to be cash sales. (p. 711)   10. _____

Part Three—Analyzing Accounts Affected by International and Internet Transactions

Directions: Analyze each of the following transactions into debit and credit parts. Print the letter identifying your choices in the proper Answers column. Determine in which journal each of the transactions is to be recorded.

G—General Journal   CP—Cash Payments Journal   CR—Cash Receipts Journal

Account Titles	Transactions	Journal	Answers Debit	Credit
A. Cash	1–2–3. Recorded an international cash sale. (p. 706)	1. _____	2. _____	3. _____
B. Sales	4–5–6. Received a time draft for an international sale. (p. 707)	4. _____	5. _____	6. _____
C. Time Drafts Receivable	7–8–9. Received cash for the value of a time draft. (p. 708)	7. _____	8. _____	9. _____
	10–11–12. Recorded Internet credit card sales. (p. 711)	10. _____	11. _____	12. _____

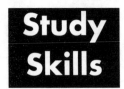

Study Skills

Preparing for Examinations

Some students seem to make poor grades anytime they take an examination. They say, "Taking an exam has always been impossible for me. I am not able to work well when there is any pressure." What they often actually mean is that they are unprepared for the exam.

Because you will take so many examinations in the future, you should do anything you can to become proficient in taking them. It is just good insurance for your future success.

Prepare Every Day

The best way to prepare for an exam is to complete every day's assignment on time. If you do, reviewing for an exam will be easy. You can review material the day before an exam, but you cannot make up for a term of neglect.

Find out when your next exam will be and pace your study so that you will have all work completed well before the exam. If there are review questions at the end of the chapters in your text, read them to determine if you know the answers. In this way, you will know if you understand the material.

Prepare Personally

You should make every effort to be prepared personally for an exam. Getting proper rest before the exam is essential. A student who arrives at the exam room sleepy and tired will not be able to do good work. Do not stay up late the evening before an exam even if you feel you need the time to study. To do well on an exam, you must be well rested and alert.

You should try to keep personal problems from interfering with your study or with your preparation for an exam. If you are concerned about a personal problem, it is difficult to concentrate your efforts on preparing for an exam.

Necessary Supplies

On the day of the exam, be sure that you have all the necessary supplies. You will likely need pens, pencils, and paper. Sometimes a special exam notebook is required.

It is a very good idea to take a watch with you to the exam so that you will be able to check the time regularly. In this way, you will not spend too much time on one part of the exam and fail to finish the entire exam.

Be Confident

If you are properly prepared, you can actually look forward to exams. Good preparation will help you to present your ideas and knowledge in the best possible way. Plan for exams and face them with confidence. You will be proud of yourself, and you will very likely make much better grades.

24-1 WORK TOGETHER, p. 709

Journalizing international sales transactions

1., 2.

CASH RECEIPTS JOURNAL

PAGE 9

	DATE	ACCOUNT TITLE	DOC. NO.	POST. REF.	GENERAL DEBIT	GENERAL CREDIT	ACCOUNTS RECEIVABLE CREDIT	SALES CREDIT	SALES DISCOUNT DEBIT	CASH DEBIT	
					1	2	3	4	5	6	
1											1
2											2
3											3
4											4
5											5
6											6
7											7
8											8
9											9
10											10

1.

GENERAL JOURNAL

PAGE 5

	DATE	ACCOUNT TITLE	DOC. NO.	POST. REF.	DEBIT	CREDIT	
					1	2	
1							1
2							2
3							3
4							4
5							5
6							6

Journalizing international sales transactions

1., 2.

CASH RECEIPTS JOURNAL

PAGE 17

DATE	ACCOUNT TITLE	DOC. NO.	POST. REF.	GENERAL DEBIT	GENERAL CREDIT	ACCOUNTS RECEIVABLE CREDIT	SALES CREDIT	SALES DISCOUNT DEBIT	CASH DEBIT	
										1
										2
										3
										4
										5
										6
										7
										8
										9
										10

1.

GENERAL JOURNAL

PAGE 9

DATE	ACCOUNT TITLE	DOC. NO.	POST. REF.	DEBIT	CREDIT	
						1
						2
						3
						4
						5
						6

24-2 WORK TOGETHER p. 712

Journalizing Internet sales transactions

1.

CASH RECEIPTS JOURNAL

PAGE 5

			1	2	3	4	5	6
			GENERAL		ACCOUNTS RECEIVABLE CREDIT	SALES CREDIT	SALES DISCOUNT DEBIT	CASH DEBIT
DATE	ACCOUNT TITLE	DOC. NO.	POST. REF.	DEBIT	CREDIT				

Journalizing Internet sales transactions

1.

CASH RECEIPTS JOURNAL

PAGE 9

DATE	ACCOUNT TITLE	DOC. NO.	POST. REF.	GENERAL DEBIT	GENERAL CREDIT	ACCOUNTS RECEIVABLE CREDIT	SALES CREDIT	SALES DISCOUNT DEBIT	CASH DEBIT	
				1	2	3	4	5	6	1
										2
										3
										4
										5
										6
										7
										8
										9
										10
										11
										12
										13
										14
										15
										16
										17
										18
										19
										20
										21
										22

24-1 APPLICATION PROBLEM, p. 714

Journalizing international sales transactions

1., 2.

CASH RECEIPTS JOURNAL

PAGE 10

		DATE	ACCOUNT TITLE	DOC. NO.	POST. REF.	GENERAL DEBIT 1	GENERAL CREDIT 2	ACCOUNTS RECEIVABLE CREDIT 3	SALES CREDIT 4	SALES DISCOUNT DEBIT 5	CASH DEBIT 6	
1												1
2												2
3												3
4												4
5												5
6												6
7												7
8												8
9												9
10												10
11												11
12												12
13												13
14												14
15												15
16												16
17												17
18												18
19												19
20												20
21												21
22												22

1.

GENERAL JOURNAL   PAGE 6

	DATE		ACCOUNT TITLE	DOC. NO.	POST. REF.	DEBIT	CREDIT	
1								1
2								2
3								3
4								4
5								5
6								6
7								7
8								8
9								9
10								10
11								11
12								12
13								13
14								14
15								15
16								16
17								17
18								18
19								19
20								20
21								21
22								22
23								23
24								24
25								25
26								26
27								27
28								28
29								29
30								30
31								31
32								32
33								33

24-2 **APPLICATION PROBLEM, p. 714**

Journalizing Internet sales transactions

1., 2.

CASH RECEIPTS JOURNAL

PAGE 15

DATE	ACCOUNT TITLE	DOC. NO.	POST. REF.	GENERAL DEBIT 1	GENERAL CREDIT 2	ACCOUNTS RECEIVABLE CREDIT 3	SALES CREDIT 4	SALES DISCOUNT DEBIT 5	CASH DEBIT 6
1									
2									
3									
4									
5									
6									
7									
8									
9									
10									
11									
12									
13									
14									
15									
16									
17									
18									
19									
20									
21									
22									

Recording international and Internet sales

1., 2.

CASH RECEIPTS JOURNAL

PAGE 2

	DATE	ACCOUNT TITLE	DOC. NO.	POST. REF.	GENERAL DEBIT	GENERAL CREDIT	ACCOUNTS RECEIVABLE CREDIT	SALES CREDIT	SALES DISCOUNT DEBIT	CASH DEBIT	
					1	2	3	4	5	6	
1											1
2											2
3											3
4											4
5											5
6											6
7											7
8											8
9											9
10											10
11											11
12											12
13											13
14											14
15											15
16											16
17											17
18											18
19											19
20											20
21											21
22											22

24-3 **MASTERY PROBLEM (concluded)**

1.

GENERAL JOURNAL   PAGE 2

	DATE	ACCOUNT TITLE	DOC. NO.	POST. REF.	DEBIT	CREDIT	
1							1
2							2
3							3
4							4
5							5
6							6
7							7
8							8
9							9
10							10
11							11
12							12
13							13
14							14
15							15
16							16
17							17
18							18
19							19
20							20
21							21
22							22
23							23
24							24
25							25
26							26
27							27
28							28
29							29
30							30
31							31
32							32
33							33

Recording international sales and converting foreign currency

1., 2.

CASH RECEIPTS JOURNAL

PAGE 11

DATE	ACCOUNT TITLE	DOC. NO.	POST. REF.	GENERAL DEBIT	GENERAL CREDIT	ACCOUNTS RECEIVABLE CREDIT	SALES CREDIT	SALES DISCOUNT DEBIT	CASH DEBIT

PRACTICE PROBLEM A-1, p. A-6

Preparing a statement of cash flows

PRACTICE PROBLEM A-2, p. A-6

Preparing a statement of cash flows